In the short space of
provides a robust, bibli
find insightful and tha
appreciation of our Re
gospel. A welcome introduction to a most important, if
often neglected Christian doctrine.

FRED G. ZASPEL,
Pastor, Reformed Baptist Church of Franconia, Pennsylvania
Executive Editor, Books At a Glance

The church needs more books addressing the topic of sin. Therefore, I am deeply thankful for this book by Dr. Iain Campbell, which gives us a solid theological introduction to the doctrine of sin. What should be a rather depressing book actually becomes a book full of hope because the author, with keen pastoral instincts, leads us to the remedy for sin found in Christ Jesus.

MARK JONES,
Minister, Faith Vancouver PCA, Vancouver, British Columbia

If we would be convinced to take the medicine, we must know the severity of our disease. In this brief but theologically robust, well-written, and much-needed book, Dr. Iain Campbell powerfully exposes the darkness of our condition in a way that makes the good news of Christ shine all the brighter.

JOEL R. BEEKE,
President, Puritan Reformed Theological Seminary,
Grand Rapids, Grand Rapids, Michigan

Countless Christians through the centuries have sought to aid all believers in their battle with the ongoing problem of sin. Like the stalwarts of old, Iain Campbell can be added to the list of those aiding us with clear and concise instruction on how to wage war with the enemy of our souls. This pocket guide will become a battle manual for any Christian desiring to yield the sword of the Spirit against the onslaughts of prevailing sin. There is no book I had rather recommend than one meant to teach believers how to daily conquer the plague of sin. This book will be a great asset to you in your daily battle."

Steven J. Lawson,
President OnePassion Ministries, Dallas, Texas

A CHRISTIAN'S POCKET GUIDE TO

SIN

THE DISEASE AND ITS CURE

IAIN D CAMPBELL

CHRISTIAN FOCUS

Unless otherwise indicated Scripture quotations are from *The Holy Bible, English Standard Version*, copyright © 2001 by Crossway Bibles, a division of Good News Publishers. Used by permission. All rights reserved. esv Text Edition: 2007.

Scripture quotations marked KJV are taken from the King James Version

Copyright © Iain D. Campbell 2015

paperback ISBN 978-1-78191-647-6
epub ISBN 978-1-78191-698-8
mobi ISBN 978-1-78191-699-5

10 9 8 7 6 5 4 3 2 1

Published by
Christian Focus Publications Ltd,
Geanies House, Fearn, Ross-shire,
IV20 1TW, Scotland, Great Britain

www.christianfocus.com

Cover design by Daniel Van Straaten

Printed by Nørhaven, Denmark

All rights reserved. No part of this publication may be reproduced, stored in a retrieval system, or transmitted, in any form, by any means, electronic, mechanical, photocopying, recording or otherwise without the prior permission of the publisher or a licence permitting restricted copying. In the U.K. such licences are issued by the Copyright Licensing Agency, Saffron House, 6-10 Kirby Street, London, EC1 8TS. www.cla.co.uk

CONTENTS

Introduction 1

1 The Bible and Sin: Identifying the disease 5

2 God and Sin:
   What the disease is doing in God's world 31

3 Man and Sin:
   How the disease affects the human experience 41

4 The Cross and Sin: Is there a cure? 69

5 The Christian and Sin:
   Applying the remedy while living with the disease 81

6 Epilogue: What's the Use of Sin? 95

   Endnotes 99

   Further Reading 103

- ⚠ Warning
- ✎ Don't Forget
- ⓘ Stop and Think
- ✸ Point of Interest

INTRODUCTION

I am aware that writing a book called 'A Pocket Guide to Sin' sounds as if I'm creating a 'how to' manual, as if this were a guide to doing wrong! Sadly, none of us needs a guide to doing wrong; we can do that perfectly well without one. Nor is my being a sinner sufficient qualification to write this little book, any more than my having an illness qualifies me to explain it.

But this is a book about an illness—a deep, universal and fatal illness called sin. Its working is lethal and toxic, and we all carry the germ. I pray that this study will help us to see the nature of that illness; but more importantly to understand the remedy that is available for us in the gospel.

Sickness is a metaphor used frequently for sin in the Bible. Isaiah's famous description of the sinful nation, for example, employs the language of sickness and disease:

> Why will you continue to rebel?
> The whole head is sick,
>   and the whole heart faint.
> From the sole of the foot even to the head,
>   there is no soundness in it,
> but bruises and sores
>   and raw wounds;
> they are not pressed out or bound up
>   or softened with oil (Isa. 1:5–6).

Jeremiah uses a similar metaphor when he asks:

> Is there no balm in Gilead?
>   Is there no physician there?
> Why then has the health of the daughter of my people
>   not been restored? (Jer. 8:22)

And Jesus himself presses the point when he was asked why he ate and drank with tax collectors and sinners:

> …Jesus answered them, 'Those who are well have no need of a physician, but those who are sick. I have not come to call the righteous but sinners to repentance' (Luke 5:31–32).

The witness of the prophets as well as the teaching of Jesus himself emphasises, therefore, that the doctrine of sin is not simply that something is wrong in the world, but that something is radically wrong in human experience. That things are wrong in the world are self-evident: all around us, as Jesus says, there is 'sexual immorality, theft, murder, adultery, coveting, wickedness, deceit, sensuality, envy, slander, pride, foolishness' (Mark 7:21–22). No one is on a campaign to build a world full of such vices; even our secular society uses the language of wickedness and of sin to describe these unpleasant aspects of our culture.

But Jesus is underlining something much more radical. These, he says, are evidences of something sinister; they are symptoms of a deeper problem. They come 'from within, out of the heart of man' (Mark 7:21). They are evidence not only that the world is not the Paradise we would wish it to be, but evidence that the heart of man is not what it ought to be. There is a pollution at the root of man's being, which is expressed in thoughts, words and actions that defile.

Against this backdrop, Jesus presents himself as the physician who can address the sickness of man's heart. That is the reason so much of Jesus' teaching was authenticated by miracles of healing; the physical healing of people was a mirror of the spiritual healing that we all need.

It is precisely for this reason that we need to have a biblical understanding of what sin is; 'sin' is the category of thought and reality which explains why the gospel is good news. Jesus died *for our sins* (1 Cor. 15:3); he was called *Jesus* 'for he will save his people from their sins' (Matt. 1:21). Sin is the problem to which the cross of Jesus is the only solution. To preach Jesus is to preach a Jesus who takes away the sin of the world (John 1:29).

To understand the gospel requires an understanding of sin. Hence this pocket-guide, in which we will try to map out the nature of the disease which only God, by his grace in Jesus Christ, is able to heal. We need to ask what the disease is, where it came from, how it is transmitted, what its effects and symptoms are. We need to know the remedy and the recovery process involved. And we need to understand that without the cure which the gospel provides, we are still 'dead in trespasses and sins' (Eph. 2:1).

The need for such knowledge could not be more acute. This is not a disease confined to one locality; it is prevalent everywhere. According to Paul, 'all have sinned' (Rom. 3:23). To state it negatively, 'none is righteous, no, not one' (Rom. 3:10, quoting Psalm 14:1). We all carry it in our hearts and it shows itself in our lives.

To be sure, this is not the only analogy which the Bible uses when it discusses the issue of sin. As we look into the nature of the disease, we will uncover some of the other descriptors used in both the Old and New Testaments for sin. But as an entry point, it is enough to know that this illness affects us all; apart from Jesus himself, there are no exceptions: 'death spread to all men, because all sinned' (Rom. 5:12).

That being so, there is nothing more glorious than God's message that 'the blood of Jesus his Son cleanses us from all sin' (1 John 1:7). We can deny the reality of sin, but by doing so 'we deceive ourselves, and the truth is not in us' (1 John 1:8). But if we confess our sin to God, we will discover the totality of his healing grace, in forgiveness and cleansing. If that is the outcome of our study of this doctrine, it will have been time well spent.

Is it possible to preach the gospel or even share it without referring to sin? Do we need to make the idea of sin more relevant for our contemporary generation?

1

THE BIBLE AND SIN

IDENTIFYING THE DISEASE

Without the Bible, we will never understand what sin is or what it does. We can talk about bad things in our lives, evil things in the world, and wicked things that people do; but we are only always dealing with symptoms. We can use psychology to explain why some people do the bad things they do; but God alone can tell us what sin is.

If we try to define sin ourselves we encounter the problem of subjectivism, where everyone makes up their own minds about what is right and what is wrong. In 2005, the UK television network Channel 4 screened two programmes on 'the ten commandments for today'. A poll was taken to see which 'ten commandments' people would have as a basic moral rule for society. The results were interesting, but the whole project was doomed to failure, since morality cannot simply be determined by a vote. One man's sin might be another man's pleasure: who is to say which is right, or which is wrong? John Lennox is absolutely right in his analysis of the new atheism that wants to say we are nothing more than a collection of cells, with no need of God to determine our behaviours: 'if there is no eternal base for values external to humanity, how can Dawkins', Hitchens', or anyone else's standards be anything but limited human conventions: ultimately meaningless products of a blind, unguided evolutionary process?'[1]

Human conventions, however, cannot define sin; only God can. We all have a sense of right and wrong, which is not a matter of culture or nature or nurture, but of creation and spirituality. The very nature of law and of morality points to a lawgiver and a moral judge. Only God can define the norms by which life ought to be lived, and he has revealed this to us in the Bible. Sometimes our definitions of what is right and what is wrong need to be re-calibrated as we listen to the Word of God. But listen we must. That is the purpose of this chapter—to try to understand the Bible's own teaching about sin.

The first explicit reference to sin in the Bible is at Genesis 4:7 in connection with Cain's murder of his brother Abel. God questioned Cain about what he had done, and, using the metaphor of an animal about to pounce, said that if he had done wrong, sin was 'crouching at the door', with a desire to have him.

The language is deliberately picturesque, illustrating the subtle, yet powerful force which had taken grasp of Cain. But sin is not simply an impersonal force, since it can never be separated from the human agent who practices it. There is such a thing as sin; and there is such a thing as a sinner. The two are to be distinguished, but are inseparable.

WORDS AND PICTURES

Before looking at the Bible's telling of how sin came into the world, it will be helpful to summarise the Bible's vocabulary for sin. Hebrew is a very poetic and pictorial language; it draws word-pictures in order to establish meanings of words. One of the most frequent Hebrew words for sin, for example (used over 500 times in the Old Testament) is borrowed from archery. The left-handed slingers of the tribe of Benjamin never missed their target (Judges 20:16), and the concept of *missing the target*—of coming short of the point at which we ought to be aiming—forms one of the basic Bible ideas about sin.

Then there are words that identify sin as a *straying from God*. Like sheep, we have wandered away from the right path (Isa. 53:6, Ps. 119:176). In the Bible sin is pictured as lostness, in which we have strayed onto dangerous paths; the counterbalance to this is that God, as the gracious shepherd of his sheep, leads them on 'paths of righteousness' (Ps. 23:2).

Sometimes the Bible describes sin with the vocabulary of *rebellion*. God warns his people not to rebel against him (Exod. 23:20), and the leaders in Israel often accuse God's people of having done exactly that (Hosea 7:14). To sin against God is to declare war on him.

There are words that identify sin as *guilt before God*. Words like 'ungodly' and 'wicked' belong to this group. To speak of men and women coming short of God's target and wandering from God's way is to strike a subjective note, and to emphasise what sin does in human experience. But more serious is the objective reality, that, having broken God's law we are accountable and guilty before him.

The New Testament uses a variety of Greek vocabulary to express the idea of sin, words which are carried over from their classical usage to the theological usage of the apostles. But they are a Greek dress on Hebrew thought, and the language of sin both in its subjective and objective aspects is carried over to the New Testament.

SIN'S ENTRY-POINT

Any understanding of sin must begin with the Bible's record of how sin entered our history. That account is given to us in Genesis 3. In spite of modern approaches to Genesis, the Bible everywhere assumes the historicity and factuality of these opening chapters. It is beyond debate for any serious reader of Scripture that God created the world, that the world was good at its point of origin, that Adam and Eve were a real couple located at a definite place at the beginning of world history, and that their lives were designed to be God-honouring, God-saturated and God-approving.[2]

In addition, the story of the fall presupposes a specific command to man. The command is explicit in Genesis 2:16–17, and centres around God's choice of a particular tree, the fruit of which Adam and Eve were forbidden to eat. The elements of the command, within a personal relationship between God and man, containing a threat for disobedience and an implied blessing for obedience, are the elements of a formal arrangement. The sin described in Genesis 3 is not just a decision on Adam's part to do something wrong, but a wilful decision to violate the formal terms of the relationship between Adam and God.

The Bible is structured around such relationships, often called 'covenants', in which two parties are bound by promises and threatenings, with God establishing the formal relationship as a means of graciously securing blessing for the other party. Although the word 'covenant' is not found in Genesis 1 or 2, the elements of the relationship are covenantal; so theologians often speak about a 'covenant of works' or a 'covenant of life' between God and man at the beginning of history.

To speak of the arrangement as a covenant of *works* is not to downplay the graciousness of God's provision; it is simply to highlight the conditionality of Adam's remaining in his innocence and happiness. To call it a covenant of *life,* as some theologies do, is to highlight the promise that obedience to God's terms would bring.

It is important to emphasise these facts, because sin does not occur in a vacuum. It occurs within relationships in which God, through sovereign grace and love, acts for the good of his world and of men and women in it. That Adam sinned is a great mystery, not least because his sin was against the backdrop of such a glorious possibility of life.

Another factor lying behind the story of the fall is the prior rebellion of Satan against God. The serpent who comes into the garden in Genesis 3:1 is the devil ('the ancient serpent' of Revelation 20:2), whose fall Jesus had witnessed (Luke 10:18). Sin had already entered the spiritual realm before it entered the physical realm of Adam's world.

Satan is the prime agent in the story of Adam's fall, and challenges the command God has given Adam. He questions whether God actually said what Adam thinks he has said (Gen. 3:1), and whether God would actually carry out the threat he had made (Gen. 3:4). By raising these doubts, Satan removes the seriousness of the choice that Adam and Eve make, with the result that they eat from the forbidden tree.

As soon as this occurs, a new realisation dawns. Although Adam and Eve have been physically naked in the garden, it was without shame or embarrassment. Now their physical nakedness seems to mirror the shame of their nakedness in the sight of God from whom they run. Summoned before God, they hear God speak to Satan, then to Eve, finally to Adam, before expelling them from Paradise.

The words of God—as he reacts against the dis-obedience of the first human couple—are a mix of judgement and of grace. There are to be far-reaching personal consequences of the sin that has just taken place; the actions inside the garden will affect everything outside of it. But grace appears in the promise that the very Satan who was the agent of rebellion will be defeated by a descendant of Eve (Gen. 3:15). Though he is expelled from the garden, Adam will be saved through hope.

One of the senior ministers in our church used to tease divinity students with the question 'What was the name of the first woman?'

The students would squirm for a moment, thinking there must be some trick, because children in Sunday School know the name of the first woman. So, they would reply: 'Eve'.

'No', he would say. 'The name of the first woman was "Woman" - she was taken from the man, and that was her name'. He was right, of course, as Genesis 2:23 explains. It was only after the fall that Adam called his wife 'Eve' (Gen. 3:20), a name that means 'living'. Her new name signified that Adam could anticipate life even though he and his wife had broken God's law.

The Bible is an extended commentary on the sin of man, revealing to us the consequences of the sin that took place in the garden of Eden, and developing the promise of a Saviour through the generations until Jesus appears to destroy the devil (Heb. 2:14, 1 John 3:8). Judgement is tempered with mercy; the consequences of sin will be played out on the stage of human history, but so too will be the consequences of grace.

So what actually happened in Eden in Genesis 3? God's law was broken, his threatened curse on disobedience became operative, and man experienced the loss of a meaningful relationship with God, with his wife and with himself. That triad of elements brings us to the heart of the Bible's theology of sin: disobedience to God's law leads to a distancing from God, and eventually brings death.

But the Bible insists that sin had a clear entry point in human experience; it was not there from the beginning. It came into man's world subsequent to his origin. God's promise also held out the reality of a terminus for sin, a defeat and an eradication of it. The Word of God tells us how the disease entered the stream of humanity; the promise of God highlights that a cure is already provided for; and the purpose of God is that it will eventually be eradicated completely.

AFTER THE FALL

The subsequent development of Old Testament history is an affirmation of the reality of Genesis 3. Paradise is lost to man; no attempt, either through relationships (as in Genesis 6:4) or through human ingenuity and ability (as in Genesis 11) can recover what has been lost through sin. As a consequence of sin, the world is marked by deprivation, dissolution and death.

God sends a universal flood as a judgement on mankind because 'the wickedness of man was great in the earth ... every intention of the thoughts of his heart was only evil continually' (Gen. 6:8). But the flood is not just a judgement on the sinfulness of man; it is also a statement on the pervasive nature of sin. If God will not destroy humankind in this way, man will destroy himself through his sin.

The reason that Noah and his family are saved is because of God's gracious covenant (Gen. 6:18). Again it is by means of a formal, covenant relationship that God will bring deliverance from sin; but it is no longer dependent on man obeying God, but on God loving man. Salvation from sin and its consequences is possible because of what God has done, and in the light of what God has promised. Man is clearly now in a different context after the fall to that in which he stood before the fall. Then, his enjoyment of life in God's presence was dependent on grace but conditioned by his obedience to God. Now, his enjoyment of life is still dependent on grace but conditioned by God's acting for him.

The theological distinction here is between the covenant of works (highlighting the relationship in which man stood to God at the beginning), and the covenant of grace (highlighting the way in which God's salvation alone can rescue man from himself and his sin). God did not need to show man mercy, but he opted to do so. There is hope, flowing from God's stated intention to rescue man out of the situation into which his disobedience had brought him.

That becomes the trajectory along which salvation will be possible: God will renew his covenant of grace with Abraham, Moses and David, until it is finally sealed and ratified as a new covenant in the blood of Jesus Christ.

The Old Testament prepares for the New, and illustrates that 'where sin increased, grace abounded all the more' (Rom. 5:20).

The idea of covenants is supremely important in the Bible. God's purpose of salvation is revealed in formal relationships in which God binds himself to people and makes them his own. That was the essence of the covenant with

- **Abraham, as we see in Genesis 12:3, 15:5, 6, 17:7**
- **Moses, as we see in Exodus 24:7-8**
- **David, as we see in 2 Samuel 7:8-13**
- **God's people in Christ, as we see in Matthew 26:28 and Hebrews 13:20**

THE LAW OF MOSES

By the time we come to the Book of Exodus, the children of Israel are slaves in Egypt, groaning to God for deliverance. The release of the Israelites is driven by God's covenant promise to Abraham (Exod. 2:24), and is further evidence of the grace of God's salvation. God judges the sin of Egypt with death, and saves his people by the substitution of a lamb. They are redeemed to be holy to the Lord.

God brings them to Mount Sinai, where he gives his people laws. Possibly no aspect of biblical theology is more debated and disputed at the present time than the law of Moses, and how it relates to the covenant of God's grace and to the believer in the New Testament. One or two preliminary points are worth making.

First, there is a clear distinction between the ten commandments of Sinai, which were written by God's finger and given special status among God's people, and the other body of law which regulated Israel's life and worship. The ten commandments represented ten absolute principles of God's Lordship over religion, worship, revelation, time, relationships, life, marriage, property, truth and the heart, and are applicable in every age and generation. The other laws of the Old Testament were specific applications of these principles to Israel as a covenant church-nation, and were temporary in duration. The ten commandments were permanent, abiding principles.

In essence, these ten words are of the same order as the prohibition God gave to Adam at the outset in the Garden of Eden. The simple command regarding forbidden fruit was also a test of Adam's commitment to God in the areas of religion, worship, revelation, time, relationships, life, marriage, property, truth and the heart. The ten commandments were, in that sense, a republication of the law God had given to man at the outset.

But it is entirely unhelpful and unbiblical to see the law of Moses, as some do, as a republication of the covenant of works, as if Israel's relationship to God was the same as Adam's. In spite of the literature generated on this subject, Israel is in the position of post-fall man everywhere: in need of saving by grace, not by works. But Israel also serves as a picture to us of the way in which

God's salvation comes to us in Christ (1 Cor. 10:11), and to that end the ten commandments do three things.

First, the commandments reveal the nature of sin as a multi-faceted reality, which introduces and insinuates itself into areas over which God has absolute supremacy and mastery. The comprehensiveness of the ten commandments is such that it leaves nothing out of God's lordship. We are accountable to him in everything.

Second, the ten commandments teach us that sin can be defined according to a moral code. If God requires something, and we do not do it, that is sin. It is not enough just to talk about things as 'sinful'. When God's law is broken, sin is committed, and the one who breaks it is a sinner. The law is the definition of what our lives should be, and how our lives should be regulated. Only one person in the whole of human history lived a life that conformed to its demands: Jesus was, and remains, the embodiment of the law. He is what we ought to have been, and what we ought to be now.

Third, the ten commandments remind us that sin leaves us accountable. Sin is not the contravention of any human code; it is a violation of the law of God. We become personally responsible before God for having broken his law.

It is important to remember, however, that the ten commandments were given to Israel within the context of God's covenant of grace, his commitment to save and redeem sinners. They are prefaced by the statement that God had redeemed his people (Exod. 20:2). As a law from God, the ten commandments are to be obeyed. They tell us how we ought to be. Therefore they also highlight for us the nature of sin, and our spiritual bankruptcy. But it is not by obeying them that we are saved; our obedience is what we all owe God, but it is as a debt to his grace that we are called to obey them.

It is easy to read passages like John 1:17 ('the law was given through Moses; grace and truth came through Jesus Christ') or Romans 6:14 ('you are not under the law but under grace') as if they taught that the law of the ten commandments is no longer binding. But that ignores the weight of the New Testament evidence; it was to these very commandments that Jesus sent the rich young ruler in Luke 18:20, where he would find the perfect revelation of God's will and goodness. Being a Christian does not mean the law doesn't matter any more; it means that we will love it more than ever.

The problem is that none of us is able to keep any of these laws perfectly. That is why the giving of the commandments is accompanied by an elaborate set of laws governing sacrifice and worship. These laws, in the wider context of the Old Testament, are not just about cultic matters; they establish the steps God is taking to deal with sin, through priestly action, atonement and intercession.

The drama and significance of these actions derives from what Jesus will do for us as the Saviour of sinners. But that is to get ahead of ourselves. We simply need to note at this point that at the heart of the Old Testament revelation of grace comes the law of the ten commandments, never repealed, which stands as the revelation of God's supreme standard, and becomes the basis of the the moral judgement which God makes on his people. As O. Palmer Robertson says, 'From the earliest era of prophets to the last, the law is applied to the people as an explanation for the judgement or blessing they may expect.'[3]

This is prominent in the historical narratives of the Old Testament also. Saul is rejected by God as king because he has not performed the commandments of God (1 Sam. 15:10). Solomon declares that there is no one who does not sin (1 Kings. 8:46), and that the wisdom of the people is to be true to the Lord 'walking in his statutes and keeping his commandments' (1 Kings 8:61). The spiritual temperature of Israel is always taken in the light of their obedience to, or deviation from, the law of God.

Perhaps no element of the Old Testament registers the personal impact of this like the Book of Psalms. From the outset, the psalmists express their delight in the law of God (Ps. 1:2), and in various ways declare the blessing of walking in God's commandments (Ps. 81:8–11; Psalm 119:1 and throughout). Yet the Psalter is also full of confession of sin (Pss. 32, 51, 130), and pleas for mercy (Ps. 57:1, 86:15, 103:8). Sin abounds in history, and in the human heart, but grace abounds all the more.

SIN AND JESUS

The first reported speech in the New Testament is the speech of the angel to Joseph:

Joseph, son of David, do not fear to take Mary as your wife, for that which is conceived in her is from the Holy Spirit. She will bear a son, and you shall call his name Jesus, for he will save his people from their sins (Matt. 1:20–21).

This speech comes in the wake of Matthew's genealogy of Jesus in Matthew 1:1–18, which has the effect of bridging the Testaments and alerting us to the Old Testament roots and foundation of all that is to follow. But the words of the angel are future: Jesus, the promised Deliverer WILL come, born of a virgin, and WILL save his people from sin.

Much of the next thirty years is passed over in silence, until the ministry of Jesus is to begin. The precursor of his ministry is that of John the Baptist, who sounds the note of repentance (Matt. 3:8), a note which will be the hallmark of Jesus' ministry too, from the opening command to 'Repent, for the kingdom of heaven is at hand' (Matt. 4:17), to its close, when he grants the disciples the authority to declare the forgiveness of sin (John 20:23).

Jesus is both declared to be, and declares himself to be, the promised, and the sole Saviour of sinners. What that means is beyond question. His coming into the world is the coming of light into the darkness (John 1:5); and although men prefer the darkness, he is able to give the light of life (John 3:19–21). He is the physician who heals the spiritually sick (Luke 5:32), the liberator who sets free sin's captives (John 8:31–34), the shepherd who recovers the lost sheep by sacrificing himself for them (Luke 15:4–7, John 10:11), the heavenly bread who feeds the dying soul (John 6:50) and the water of life who quenches the deepest thirst (John 4:13–14; 7:37). The constant theme of Jesus' ministry is the depth of the world's need and the sufficiency of the depth of God's grace.

We will deal in a subsequent chapter with how it is that Jesus is able to meet the needs of sinners. But a close examination of his teaching reveals several things.

First, the teaching of Jesus highlights the fact that sin is a *universal phenomenon*. The world is a dark and dying world, and it needs Jesus' gospel. By saying that he had not come to call the righteous but sinners, Jesus is not implying that there are some who do not require his ministry and mission. The 'righteous' are those who are well enough in their own eyes. They need to be convicted of their sin—a point which Jesus says will come with the ministry of the Holy Spirit (John 16:8–9). All are in darkness, and gravitate naturally towards it (John 3:19).

Second, the teaching of Jesus shows that sin is a radical *state of enslavement*. The Jewish leaders objected to this emphasis, arguing that as the offspring of Abraham they had never been the slaves of any (John 8:32). But Jesus' point is well established; refusal to come to him is itself both a sin and the result of sin (John 5:40). Deeper still, the tyranny of sin manifests itself in the bondage of the human will: no-one, says Jesus, 'can come to me unless the Father who sent me draws him' (John 6:44). The passage from Isaiah 61, with which Jesus inaugurates his ministry, is not so much a programme for liberation theology as a statement of the spiritual realities which Christ has come to effect: he will set (spiritual) prisoners free (Isa. 61:1–2, cited in Luke 4:18).

Third, Jesus teaches that sins *may be forgiven*; indeed, he shows that he has the power to forgive them. His miracles of healing are directly related to the restoration of spiritual life through the forgiveness of sins; the healing of the paralysed man, for example, has as its stated purpose 'that you may know that the Son of Man has authority on earth to forgive sins' (Matt. 9:6). The miracles authenticate the ministry of Christ, and are their own apologia for his saving mission.

There is in these miracles, therefore, a radical eschatological dimension. Sin means that communion with God has been broken, and the world's equilibrium has been compromised. Instead of the life and blessing of Eden, there is brokenness, illness and death. The mission of Jesus has as its aim that at last Paradise will be restored, and there will be no more decay or disease. That can only be accomplished through dealing with the problem of sin, which is in his power to forgive. The only sin that cannot be forgiven is a sin of blasphemy against the Holy Spirit (Matt. 12:31–32, Mark 3:28–30), which is a dogged refusal to yield to the saving power of Jesus Christ.

The unforgivable sin of which Jesus speaks in Matthew 12 and Mark 3 has caused endless discussion. What do you understand this sin to be? How does it manifest itself? How would you advise a person who thinks they may be guilty of it?

Did Jesus teach about the unforgivable sin in order to discourage people from believing in him?

In all of this, we have a living embodiment in Jesus himself of what it is to live in full conformity to the claims of God, and therefore to live the life of Heaven on earth. He is the embodiment of God's law, of whom it is true, as one of his closest disciples testified, that 'he committed no sin, neither was deceit found in his mouth' (1 Pet. 2:22). To use B.B. Warfield's famous illustration, he is the moral plumb-line which reveals how crooked humanity has become: 'men are revealed in his presence in their true, their fundamental natural tones, with a vivid completeness in which they are never seen elsewhere.'[4]

THE REST OF THE NEW TESTAMENT

The gospels and Acts are a historical narrative which lays the foundation for the doctrine set forth in the epistles. They are of a piece; the claims of modern scholarship that the religion and faith of Jesus is different to that of Paul cannot be defended. The apostles, including Paul, continue the teaching of the Lord. The Book of Acts, for example, continues the same theme of salvation as grounded solely in Jesus Christ (Acts 4:12), and calls all men everywhere to repent and believe (Acts 2:38; 3:19; 17:30; 26:20).

But it is in the letters of the New Testament that we have a fully developed biblical doctrine of sin, particularly in Paul's letter to the Romans. Romans is an extended New Testament sermon on an Old Testament text. The text is Habakkuk 2:4, 'the righteous shall live by faith' (cited in Romans 1:17), and it begs two questions: who are the righteous? and what is the faith by which they shall live?

The answer to the first of these questions is what requires Paul to deal with the meaning and nature of sin. Righteousness is the opposite of sin. If sin means deviation and coming short of God's standard, righteousness is the state of conformity to it. Righteousness is more than innocence; it is a continual meeting of God's requirements and an incessant obedience to God's law.

As Paul is at pains to point out in the opening chapters of Romans, righteousness is the one thing we all need, and the one thing we cannot supply for ourselves. Common to us all, to Jews (who first received the light of the gospel) and to Gentiles (the non-Jewish world who did not have the Bible): 'all, both Jews and Greeks, are under sin' (Rom. 3:9).

Paul begins with the Gentiles, presumably because it is to Gentiles he is writing, and argues that even without the written revelation of law they are guilty before God. God's existence is evident in the glory and beauty of creation, but people choose to live as if there were no God (Rom. 1:20). For this, there is no excuse. But religious privileges will not save either; to boast in the outward trappings of our religion is vain. The true child of God is not one who has been brought into the covenant by external rites, like circumcision, but whose heart has been changed by God's Spirit (Rom. 3:29). This note is consistent with the emphasis throughout the Old Testament that it is to the heart God looks (Deut. 10:16, Jer. 4:4).

> The ways in which Paul describes the sin of the Jewish world in Romans 2 can be applied to Gentiles too. He is saying that it is not enough to have the outward ceremonies and rituals of the church applied to us; we need to be Christians in the heart, not just in our religious duties. Try reading Romans 2:25-29, for example, substituting 'Christian' for 'Jew' and 'baptism' for circumcision'!

Paul brings his discussion of the nature of sin to its central and key point: we have fallen and sinned in Adam. Romans 5:12–21 is a fundamental part of Paul's doctrine of sin. It was through one man (Adam) that sin came into the world, and death passed on all men. But the reason all die is because of a solidarity that all mankind has with Adam. Before the Mosaic law was given, all sinned. Not all were presented with a revelation of God's will, as Adam was by God's speech, and Israel by God's writing; but all sinned nonetheless.

The reason for this is that we all stand in relation to Adam the way Christians stand in relation to Christ. Adam was 'a type of the one who was to come' (Rom 5:14). Just as Jesus took our place on the cross, representing us before God so that what he did and suffered was for us and for our salvation, so Adam was in our place at the beginning, representing us before God. What he did in the garden was for us, and had the potential either to confirm us in our blessedness or forfeit our enjoyment of the blessing and favour of God. By disobeying God, Adam did more than lose God's blessing himself; his one act of disobedience 'led to condemnation for all men' (Rom 5:16).

There is a similarity between Adam and Christ in that both were representative men. God's formal, covenant relationship, by which life and blessing could be secured, was through Adam at the beginning and Christ in the end. They were the men through whom covenant privileges and opportunities were mediated to those in whose place they transacted with God. But there is a contrast in the outcomes and effects of the two men: whereas Adam's disobedience led to death, Christ's obedience leads to righteousness.

On the one hand we have a works-orientated covenant which offered mankind, in Adam, the opportunity to have life and blessedness in God's presence. But Adam sinned, and we sinned in him. For this reason we are in a state of spiritual death. That is the state of sin.

On the other hand we have a grace-orientated covenant which offers mankind, in Christ, the opportunity to have life and blessedness restored and enjoyed in God's presence. Christ obeyed, and faith in him means receiving the benefits of his obedience ourselves. Through his perfect obedience we may be 'justified' (Rom. 5:1), that is, declared in the light of the law to be innocent and free of the penalty. That is the state of righteousness. We can only be in a state of sin, or in a state of righteousness.

In Romans, Paul emphasises his key and central doctrine—that it is by being united with Christ that we have salvation. Through this union, the power of sin is defeated because we have died and risen with Christ. By that same union we have new life through the Spirit of God, and can live to God's glory. As Paul puts it in Ephesians 2:4–8:

> But God, who is rich in mercy, for his great love wherewith he loved us, even when we were dead in sins, hath quickened us together with Christ, (by grace ye are saved;) And hath raised us up together, and made us sit together in heavenly places in Christ Jesus: That in the ages to come he might shew the exceeding riches of his grace in his kindness toward us through Christ Jesus. For by grace are ye saved through faith; and that not of yourselves: it is the gift of God.

What we lost through our fall is restored to us in union with the living, risen Christ. The extreme nature of the condition of sin is expressed by Paul in the language of death and resurrection. Only a power equal to the power of Christ's physical resurrection will be adequate to effect a spiritual resurrection in our souls. That power is ours through union with Jesus Christ.

The emphasis of the New Testament is that without the work of Jesus, our sins would be against us; our condition would be unchanged and our guilt undiminished. The letter to the Hebrews insists that it was to deal with sin that Christ did all that he did. He has purged our sins (Heb 1:3). He has made reconciliation for the sins of the people (Heb 2:17). He was offered once to bear the sins of many (Heb 9:26–8). The ritual of priesthood and sacrifice in the Old Testament derives from the work of Jesus as our great priest, and is to be understood in the light of the cross.

Peter also highlights this in his emphasis on our salvation. Jesus has redeemed us by his blood, the blood of a spotless lamb (1 Pet. 1:18–19), a doctrine which has particular reference to the redemption of God's people from Egypt through the death of a substitutionary lamb whose blood is sprinkled on the homes of God's people (Exod. 12:5;13). More explicitly, Peter says that Jesus carried our sins in his own body on the cross (1 Pet. 2:24), so that in some sense our sins were made his, in a way that did not compromise his own sinlessness and impeccability, but enabled him to stand accountable for them. The New Testament doctrine, which parallels the teaching both of the gospels and of Paul, is that 'Christ also suffered once for sins, the righteous for the unrighteous, that he might bring us to God, being put to death in the flesh but made alive in the spirit' (1 Pet. 3:18).

The same note is found in the epistles of John. Through the blood of Jesus, sins may be cleansed (1 John 1:7), since he is the 'propitiation' (the wrath-averting sacrifice) for our sins (1 John 2:1). Interestingly too, John gives a clear and straightforward definition of sin as *lawlessness* (1 John 3:4), a concept which not only defines sin as disobedience to God's law but, in its very nature an anomaly, something which ought not to be.

The ultimate eradication of sin from God's universe, as well as from the experience of God's people, is the stated hope of the New Testament. We are looking, says Peter, 'for new heavens and a new earth in which righteousness dwells' (2 Pet. 3:11). This is the vision John sees in Revelation concerning the heavenly and renewed Jerusalem, of which we read that 'nothing unclean will ever enter it, nor anyone who does what is detestable or false, but only those who are written in the Lamb's book of life' (Rev. 21:27). Paradise is ultimately restored and regained, never to be lost again, while the consequences of sin for those who refuse to trust in Jesus are eternal death and separation from God.

WHAT IS SIN?

The Westminster Shorter Catechism famously asks the question, 'What is sin?', and responds with the words, 'Sin is any want [lack] of conformity unto, or transgression of, the law of God' (Shorter Catechism, Q14). It is as succinct an answer as one could possibly give in the light of the biblical data. Sin cannot exist in the absence of law (Rom. 5:13), and glad and willing obedience to God's law is the highest service we can render to him.

But we have failed to render such service to him. That is what sin means, and we are all implicated. As we summarise this survey of biblical material, there are three things we can say about the meaning of sin.

First, *sin rebels against God's expressed and stated will.*

The relationship of sin to the will of God is something we will discuss later. But if God's law means anything it means that he reveals to us what he wants us to do. He makes his will known. He made it known to Adam. He made it known to Israel in the law. He makes it known in the teachings of Jesus Christ. If we love God in Christ, we will keep his commandments. Obedience and love are not at all exclusive of one another. Indeed, love is the fulfilling of the law (Rom. 13:10).

But sin means a direct or indirect contravention of God's standard. We both fail to do what God requires, and we choose to do what God forbids. Either way, sin always has reference to God. It is a statement of our condition in relation to our Creator, Lawgiver and King, to whom we owe loyalty and obedience. Sin means we rebel against his authority and set ourselves up as monarchs in his place.

Second, *sin overthrows God's design for the world.*

If the first is true, the second follows. All law is passed with a good intention. Rules of football are designed to make the game enjoyable and fulfilling. Rules of driving are designed to make the roads safe. Rules are there for the best intention and outcome.

God's laws are not arbitrary. They were given to man in innocence before the fall in order that man would continue to enjoy God and give him glory. They were given to man in sin as an expression of grace, to show the arena within which man, trusting to God's covenant promise, could know fellowship and blessing. God's law is perfect, and keeping it is its own reward (Ps. 19:7, 11). His design in giving it is a good one, for the benefit of man and his world.

But sin spoils, mars and ruins God's world. It attempts to redesign and recalibrate. It sets new parameters and sets new goals. It makes man the centre of all things, and his word the final judge. The result is chaos, dissatisfaction and death. Sin is a de-creating of God's world.

Third, *sin contradicts the example of Jesus Christ.*

Only one man maintained a life of spotless integrity: Jesus Christ, the Messiah-Saviour of God's providing. Isaiah predicted of him that he would magnify God's law and make it glorious (Isa. 42:21). That is the meaning of righteousness: Jesus did nothing that contradicted or transgressed the law of God in any particular. His obedience is our merit before God.

To sin, therefore, is to live a life that is unlike that of Jesus, who left us an example, to walk in his steps (1 Pet. 2:21). He could say that he always did the things that were pleasing to God (John 8:29), and that standard of living is to be replicated in us (Eph. 5:10). To return to our original analogy, to be spiritually healthy is to be like Jesus. To be spiritually unwell, because of sin, is to need him as our Saviour.

> **In the light of the biblical teaching on sin, is the Shorter Catechism right? Is sin 'any want of conformity unto, or transgression of, the law of God'?**

2

GOD AND SIN

WHAT THE DISEASE IS DOING IN GOD'S WORLD

Before we go any further into looking at the nature of sin and what it has done in our human experience we need to ask about God's own relationship to sin. After all, if he created a holy human race in a good world, why did he allow sin to come in to spoil their existence? If God is all-knowing, sin was no surprise to him. If God is sovereign over all things, does that mean that he decreed sin? Or permitted it? Or both? If God is all-powerful, could he have set up things in some other way, so as to create a world in which there would never be any sin?

Does it not seem strange that God allowed sin to come into the world and then made a plan to rescue man?

Might he not have prevented sin in the first place? Or was his plan the reverse? Did he plan to save man and then allow the Fall into sin as a means to that end? And if so, what kind of God is he?

These questions have been asked by theologians down through the centuries. Tertullian, for example, one of the church fathers from the late second to early third centuries, engages with Marcion (a heretic who rejected the Old Testament) and discusses at length the relationship between the sovereign purpose of God and the free will of man. Tertullian argues that we must begin with God's *goodness*, displayed in the many gifts which he put at man's disposal; then we must distinguish God's *purpose*, which God displayed by endowing man with free will. Tertullian concludes by stating that 'the goodness of God, then fully considered from the beginning of His works, will be enough to convince us that nothing evil could possibly have come forth from God; and the liberty of man will, after a second thought, show us that it alone is chargeable with the fault which itself committed.'[5]

But Tertullian has then to explain how God would not have been good had he taken man's free choice away. God knew, says Tertullian, 'that man would make a bad use of his created constitution; and yet what can be so worthy of God as his earnestness of purpose….?'[6] So 'if it is man's sin, it will not be God's fault, because it is man's doing; nor is that Being who be regarded as the author of the sin, who turns out to be its forbidder….'[7]

Tertullian is important not only because he shows that these difficult issues were being grappled with within two hundred years of the Bible being completed, but because in many ways he is the father of Western theology. He lays an important foundation for subsequent reflection on this theme of the relationship between the nature of God and the presence of sin and evil in the world.

It is a theme which no attempt at theology—at systematising the information of the Bible—can ignore. As Alister McGrath says, the existence of evil presents us with 'a major problem which concerns the doctrine of God.'[8] We freely concede that the problem is not God's; what is to us the 'mystery of lawlessness' (2 Thess. 2:7) is no mystery to God. But it is a mystery to us, and no small part of it is the relationship between God and evil. The technical term for a theological statement of that relationship is 'theodicy'.

As early as Genesis 45 the Bible itself gives us a theodicy. Joseph has been sold into Egyptian slavery as a result of cruel betrayal by the very brothers who ought to have protected him. By a series of tests they come to acknowledge their guilt (Gen. 44:16), and the time is now opportune for Joseph to reveal his true identity. His interpretation of God's will and providence in the matter is so remarkable as to absolve the brothers of the deed which they perpetrated: 'it was not you who sent me here but God' he says in Genesis 45:8. Of this remarkable passage John Calvin says that we are instructed 'in what manner and for what purpose we must consider the providence of God,'[9] and he goes on to emphasise that it was not by a mere permission but by his determinate counsel and will these things happen. The sin is the sin of the brothers; but, says Calvin, 'God works wonderfully through their means, in order that, from their impurity, he may bring forth his perfect righteousness.'[10] To which he adds that 'this method of acting is secret, and far above our understanding'.

This latter principle is important. The mind of God is far above our capacity to understand. It is in this light that we must read passages like Proverbs 16:4—'The Lord has made everything for its purpose, even the wicked for the day of trouble', or Isaiah 45:7, where God says 'I form light and create darkness, I make well-being and create calamity (lit. 'evil'). We have to begin with God's sovereign decree and his work of providence, which are over all. As Geerhardus Vos says, 'the difference cannot be as if evil were decreed by God with less firmness. Everything is equally firm. Something is decreed or it is not decreed, and a third supposedly lying in between may not be entertained.'[11]

The cross of Christ is our definitive entry-point into this mystery. Peter makes this profound statement on

---

There is always an element of mystery to faith. And no mystery is greater than why God should allow sin, with its subsequent miseries of sickness, disaster and death.

But we should not confuse what is ABOVE reason with what is AGAINST reason. Our minds may not be able to reach to the heights of God's knowledge, but that does not mean that our faith is unreasonable. Indeed, if our reflection on God and his ways does not leave us crying out 'O the depth of the riches and wisdom and knowledge of God! How unsearchable are his judgements and how inscrutable are his ways!' (Rom. 11:33), then we have failed to turn our theology into doxology.

the day of Pentecost, as he brings the full weight of culpability to bear on the Jewish leaders who rejected and crucified Jesus:

> …this Jesus, delivered up according to the definite plan and foreknowledge of God, you crucified and killed by the hands of lawless men (Acts 2:23).

There are two emphases here. First, *the cross was determined by God himself*. It was not just that he permitted it, but that he ordained it as something that must take place. It could not not happen. God foresaw it happening, and he allowed it to happen, but he decreed its occurrence. Jesus was crucified because God willed it so. There is a vertical dimension to the cross in which its happening was entirely purposed. It was the will of God to crush him (Isa. 53:10).

Second, *the cross was a sinful, wicked act*. It was an act of defiance, of lawlessness and of rebellion against God. An innocent man was put on a cross. By no law of justice could that act be justified. More importantly, by no theology of divine decree or of divine providence could the sinfulness of the act be justified. The sin was that of the perpetrators who twisted the judicial proceedings and therefore engineered an execution that was entirely unworthy and undeserving. There is also, therefore, a horizontal dimension to the cross in which it ought never to have happened at all. If the rulers had understood this, 'they would not have crucified the Lord of glory' (1 Cor. 2:8).

From these twin emphases of Peter's statement several conclusions follow. First, *the sin of the cross was in the mind of God before it was in the minds of men*. By extension, the sin of the Fall was in the mind of God before it was in the mind of Satan, of Eve or of Adam. And the sins of our lives are in the mind of God before they enter ours. Whether we come at this from the point of view of God foreseeing, permitting or decreeing sin, the reality, according to Scripture, is that God's mind knew the sin before anyone else's did.

Second, *the sin of the cross was willed by God as a possibility*. Sin is the very opposite—the very antithesis—of what God is, yet he willed the possibility of what is opposite to himself. Herman Bavinck is very helpful here:

> It was not Satan, nor Adam and Eve, who first conceived the idea of sin: God himself as it were made it visible to their eyes ... before the fall he even permitted an evil power from without to insinuate itself into Paradise, using the snake as its medium, and to discuss with Eve the meaning of the probationary command. There is therefore no doubt that God willed the possibility of sin.[12]

Third, *the cross was decreed in terms of all the providences and circumstances that led up to it*, including those of its perpetrators, and their own individual free choices. No one who crucified Jesus was forced to do so against their will. Light came into the world, and men preferred darkness (John 3:19). God's decree extends to all the events that anticipated the crucifixion, so that nothing was left to chance.

Fourth, *the cross did not occur by God's permission only*. The language of Peter is absolute: it was by God's 'determinate counsel' (KJV) that Jesus was crucified, not by his bare permission. He did not, in other words, simply allow wicked men to crucify his Son; he actually determined that it should be so.

Fifth, *the sinfulness of the cross was not decreed by God*. God willed its occurrence, but not the sin of its occurrence. In the same way, God ordained the Fall, but not the sinfulness of the Fall. If there is blame to be apportioned, and if guilt follows, it falls entirely on those who, with wicked hands, crucified the Lord of glory. The sinfulness of our sin is the reason we need to repent of it, and that arises from our will, not God's.

Sixth, *the decree of God means that the sinful crucifixion of Jesus is accommodated into God's plan and overruled for God's glory*. That is the point at which we must locate sin within the circle of theology. As Bavinck says, 'it is precisely God's greatness to so rule and overrule sin that against its own genius and intent it becomes serviceable to the honour of his name.'[13] That neither justifies nor explains sin; it does not provide it with an excuse, nor does it give it a rationale. But it does remind us that the naked statement of Scripture that 'the Lord reigns' (Ps. 93:1) includes in it the fact that he reigns in absolute sovereignty over the sin of man.

The cross of Calvary was God's act as well as man's act. Our preaching of the crucifixion must do justice to both. God's purpose of salvation does not detract from man's purpose of sin in nailing Jesus to the cross.

CONFESSING GOD'S SOVEREIGNTY

The *Westminster Confession of Faith* addresses the question of God's sovereignty over sin in its discussion 'Of God's Eternal Decree'. The chapter opens by stating that

> *God from all eternity, did, by the most wise and holy counsel of His own will, freely, and unchangeably ordain whatsoever comes to pass; yet so, as thereby neither is God the author of sin, nor is violence offered to the will of the creatures; nor is the liberty or contingency of second causes taken away, but rather established* (WCF 3.1).

The primary statement of this confession is a reminder to us that everything takes place under, and as a result of, God's absolute and sovereign control. It is a restating of the truth of Ephesians 1:11, that God 'works all things according to the counsel of his will'. There is nothing outwith the scope of the 'all things'. Sin is worked out according to the counsel of God's will. To confess otherwise would be to say that there are areas of life that are outwith the control of God.

But immediately the Confession makes three qualifying statements. The first is that 'God is not the author of sin'. Man is the author of his own sin, even although God authored its possibility and decreed its actuality. The second is that man's freedom is nowhere compromised by God's sovereignty. God is absolutely free. Man is relatively free, bound by the limitations of his power and compromised now by the fact of sin itself. But no-one can say that the decree or sovereignty of God forced them to sin. The third qualifier is that God's sovereignty does not remove secondary causes. God, as we have noted, willed the crucifixion of Jesus, thereby establishing every human means employed to that end. Coincidences and seemingly chance occurrences are ordered within the scope of God's decree. We are God's sinners. But our sin is our own.

These, as Chad Van Dixhoorn says, 'are deep waters, and we admit that we only splash in the shallows of theology.'[14] But splash we must if we are to confess the Bible's teaching both that all things are from God, through God, and to God (Rom. 11:36), and that in him there is no darkness at all (1 John 1:5). The fitting response to the mystery of God's sovereign decree, as it includes every event, and ultimately issues in the predestination to life of unworthy sinners, is to ascribe to him all the glory and the praise: 'the contemplation of God in this great and high mystery results in an overwhelming sense of reverence.'[15]

So what are we to say about God's relation to human sin, whether to the Fall or to the crucifixion or to our own sins? Robert L. Dabney summarises the biblical position well:

The act is man's alone, though its occurrence is efficaciously secured by God. And the sin is man's only. God's concern in it is holy, first, because all His personal agency in arranging to secure its occurrence was holy; and second, His ends or purposes are holy. God does not will the sin of the act, for the sake of its sinfulness; but only wills the result to which the act is a means, and that result is always worthy of his holiness.[16]

That is where we must begin and end, in worship of the God who acts and reacts in a way that is always consistent with his own holiness. Seen in that light, sin is that which ought not to exist at all; that it does is decreed by God, and its blameworthiness falls entirely on us.

3

MAN AND SIN

HOW THE DISEASE AFFECTS THE HUMAN EXPERIENCE

The Bible gives us a definition of sin as a power in human life that is pervasive and thoroughgoing. But we must now explore, in the light of the Bible's teaching, how the disease of sin spreads through the generations. Do we all begin as Adam began, in innocence, with the power to choose between the absolute alternatives of good and evil? Or is there, to use the language of theology, such a thing as *original* sin, meaning that sin is present with us from the point of our origin?

There are six main points to consider in this section of our study.

SIN'S ORIGIN IN HUMAN EXPERIENCE

We have already noted that the Bible shows a point of entry for sin into human history. The primitive goodness of man was lost by the fall of Adam, and cannot be regained except through Christ. But there are at least three theological implications of this.

First, from the moment sin entered into Adam's life it entered into the life of Everyman. This is the teaching of Romans 5:12–14:

> Therefore, just as sin came into the world though one man, and death through sin, and so death spread to all men because all sinned—for sin indeed was in the world before the law was given, but sin is not counted where there is no law. Yet death reigned from Adam to Moses, even over those whose sinning was not like the transgression of Adam, who was a type of the one who was to come.

This latter section of Romans 5 is in some way a parenthesis. Having established that we are justified freely by God's grace (3:24) on the basis of Christ's blood (5:9) and solely through faith, without any contribution or merit of our own (5:1), Paul has concluded that the totality of our salvation is bound up in the death and subsequent life of Jesus Christ.

It is now necessary for Paul to show that the human race is saved on the same basis upon which it was ruined—by God dealing with one representative man whose response to God's will will have consequences for all those on whose behalf he acts. God dealt with

Adam not in a private capacity only, but in a public, representative, covenant capacity. If Adam were not the representative of the race, how else could his sin bring death on all? At the level of representation he is a 'type', or symbolic foreshadowing, of Jesus, who was to come (Rom. 5:14).

This is the explanation of the matrix of sin and death which engulfed and enfettered Adam's immediate descendants, up to the point at which the law was given by Moses. The important principle obtains that where there is no law there can be no sin, for sin, as we have seen, is law-breaking. But sin is in the world, and death is in the world, even in the post-Fall period prior to the giving of the law, as a consequence of the sin of Adam. In that period death spread (Rom. 5:12, highlighting the contagious nature of the disease), and death reigned (Rom. 5:14, 17).

It was not necessary for every one of Adam's sons to have been given the same prohibition as he was given; they were not innocent as he was when they came into existence. Quite the contrary: they were already implicated in *his* sin; his 'one trespass' led to 'condemnation for all men' (Rom. 5:18).

In reality, we have only one of two alternatives: either we come into the world innocent or guilty. We can look at a little child and talk of innocence from the point of view of the incapacity and incapability of the child to perform any obvious acts of wickedness. But leave the child to his or her own devices and it is not innocence that will manifest itself, but sin. Our children do not require to be taught how to misbehave, but to be corrected and taught to do what is right. We are all born into a compromised race, already under guilt and condemnation.

Second, the infection of sin is bound up with the biological and procreative process by which the human race is perpetuated.

It is true that in Romans 5:12–17, although Paul makes a connection between Adam's sin and ours:

> (he) says nothing explicitly about *how* the sin of one man, Adam, has resulted in death for everyone .. What he *has* made clear is that the causal nexus between sin and death, exhibited in the case of Adam, has repeated itself in the case of every human being.[17]

But the Bible does not leave us to speculate on this. David, for example, expresses the guilt of his sin not merely in terms of the actual deeds he performed, but in terms of his sinful nature: *Behold, I was brought forth in iniquity, and in sin did my mother conceive me* (Ps. 51:1).

He is not speaking here of the sin of his mother in conceiving him, but in his own sinfulness at the point of his conception. David is acknowledging that the sin which he has committed has arisen out of the fallenness of his own nature. He is not thereby excusing it; quite the contrary—he is seeing that the root of it is deep within his own being, and confessing not only the sinful act which he perpetrated, but the sinful nature out of which it arose.

In his treatment of original sin, Jonathan Edwards turns our attention to the words of Jesus in John 3:6,

'That which is born of the flesh is flesh, and that which is born of the Spirit is spirit'. There is a distinction, he argues, between the first birth and the second, or the new, birth; and the necessity of the new birth is grounded in the differing nature of both of these births. If all that Jesus meant by saying 'that which is born of the flesh is flesh' was that humans beget humans, then he would merely be stating the obvious, and the contrast between flesh and Spirit would be unnecessary. But Jesus' manner of stating this antithesis, says Edwards,

> implies that what is born in the first birth of man, is nothing but man as he is of himself, without anything divine in him; depraved, debased, sinful, ruined man, utterly unfit to enter into the kingdom of God, and incapable of the spiritual divine happiness of that kingdom. But that which is born in the new birth, of the Spirit of God, is a spiritual principle, a holy and divine nature, meet for the heavenly kingdom.[18]

The point that Jesus makes is that the two births yield two different types of man. In our first birth, sin is with us at the point of our origin. If that is all we have, we are unfit for the kingdom of heaven. In the second birth, grace is with us at the point of our origin. If we have this, we have everything.

To some people the idea of original sin is offensive and repugnant. But as a doctrine it safeguards two important principles. The first is that God sees us not only in the light of what we are and have done, but in the light of what we were and ought to have been. In the language of W.G.T. Shedd:

> When God forms his estimate of man's obligations, when he lays judgement to the line and righteousness to the plummet he goes back to the beginning; he goes back to creation, and demands from his rational and immortal creature that perfect service which he was capable of rendering by creation, but which now he is unable to render because of subsequent apostasy. For God cannot adjust his demands to the alterations which sinful man makes in himself.[19]

Our sin is judged against the ultimate standard of God's image in us, and not against the standard of our human image compared with others.

The second principle is the nature of our fallenness. It is not merely the sinful acts which we perform that leave us guilty before God, but the corrupt spring out of which they come: what King Solomon powerfully describes as 'the plague of the heart' (1 Kings. 8:38, KJV). In the succinct language of B.B. Warfield, 'by original sin we are to mean not merely adherent but also inherent sin, not merely the sinful act of Adam imputed to us, but also the sinful state of our own souls conveyed to us by the just judgement of God.'[20]

Warfield is dealing with the nature of true repentance, and argues that it must include repentance for the sin that *inheres* as well as for the sin that *adheres*. We feel the guilt and shame of actual transgressions, but until we have felt that sin truly dwells in us we cannot properly repent. So the disease is in us from the point of our biological origin.

Third, sin remains a personal reality, but is not part of the definition of our humanness. To be human does not require us to be sinful. Quite the opposite. Sin is what dehumanises us. We were made for the glory of God, and sin means that we come short of the glory of God (Rom. 3:23). It is an unmaking of ourselves, a deconstructing of man.

That this is so is evident in the fact that Jesus was without sin. The Bible is clear on that fact. Jesus did no sin (1 Pet. 2:22). He knew no sin (2 Cor. 5:21). In him was no sin (1 John 3:5). Yet he was perfectly human, made like his brothers in every way, sin excepted (Heb. 2:17). Like them, he was not without temptation. But unlike them, he was without sin.

For this reason the Bible is careful in its delineation of the person of Jesus. For example, in Romans 8:3 Paul describes Jesus as being sent by God 'in the likeness of sinful flesh'. There are two components to this description. Jesus does not appear in the likeness of flesh, for that would make him other than human. But nor does he appear in sinful flesh, for that would make him incapable of answering for our sins before God. He is said to appear *in the likeness of sinful flesh*, because he came as a real man to deal with a human catastrophe, that those who stood condemned by sinful flesh might be saved.

Man is noble and good, the crown of God's creation. The work of the Spirit of God in the world is such that he can perform noble deeds, just as surely as he can perform base sins. But the goodness is the result of God's actions, not ours. For, left to ourselves, we would create hell on earth.

Sin has so modified our humanness that we have all turned aside from God, with the venom of asps on our tongue and our feet swift to shed blood (see Romans 3:13, 15). We are human, to be sure; but we are also corrupted in our nature. Sinfulness must be distinguished from humanness, but the Fall of man is such that now there is no possibility of any of us recognising or being human and not sinful. How did such a disease as this get passed on to us?

Are we sinners because we sin?

or

Do we sin because we are sinners?

SIN'S TRANSMISSION IN HUMAN EXPERIENCE

The answer of the Bible is in terms of *imputation*. When something is 'imputed' to someone, it is reckoned to them, held to be theirs. In his glossary of special theological terms, Wayne Grudem defines 'to impute' as 'to think of as belonging to someone, and therefore to cause it to belong to that person.'[21] Imputation, says B.B. Warfield 'is simply the act of setting to one's account; and the act of setting to one's account is in itself the same act whether the thing set to his account stands on the credit or debit side of the account, and whatever may be the ground in equity on which it is set to his account.'[22]

It may seem strange—even unfair—that one person's sin should be regarded as someone else's. But the Bible does not treat the human race as an collection of individuals, but as an organic unity, all in solidarity with the first man, Adam. Scripture only teaches what we, as human beings, experience and observe: that we are all implicated in sin. It is a trait common to every member of the human family. To use the words of Herman Bavinck, 'every human is born under a moral debt. That debt is not something each one of us has—personally, individually, actually—brought down on ourselves. It rests on each one of us on account of Adam.'[23]

But how does it rest on us? There have been various answers to that question, both based on the concept of imputation. W.G.T. Shedd, for example, argues that 'The *total* guilt of the first sin, thus committed by the entire race in Adam, is imputed to each individual of the race because of the *indivisibility* of guilt.'[24] This imputation rests, according to Shedd, on the natural union we have with Adam, 'a union of constitutional nature and substance.'[25] Because we are of the same human substance with Adam, and are one with him in constitution, his sin is necessarily imputed to all those who are descended from him. This is sometimes called the realist view of imputation.

Charles Hodge does not wish to downplay the natural union we have with Adam, but wants to do justice to the covenant framework within which that union takes place. It is not only that we are one with Adam in substance; our union with Adam, he says, is both 'federal and natural' (federal meaning covenantal).[26] The result is that Adam's sin, 'although not their act, is so imputed to them that it is the judicial ground of the penalty threatened against him coming also upon them.'[27] This is described as 'immediate imputation'. Our carnal union with Adam, together with Adam's representative character, means that both his corruption and his guilt are ours.

Another position taught that what is imputed to us is only a corrupt nature, and not the guilt of Adam's sin. We are considered guilty because we are corrupt. This view was first advanced in France, and came into New England theology through the philosophical theology of Jonathan Edwards. In its most basic form, this view taught that we inherit our fallen nature by imputation from Adam, but not its guilt. This is the view known as mediate imputation.

The Helvetic Consensus of 1675 (under the influence of leading Reformed theologians such as Francis Turretin) decisively rejected mediate imputation, and summarised the biblical position in the following statement:

> For a double reason, therefore, man, because of sin, is by nature, and hence from his birth, before committing any actual sin, exposed to God's wrath and curse; first, on account of the transgression and disobedience which he committed in the loins of Adam; and, secondly, on account of the consequent hereditary corruption implanted to his very conception, whereby his whole nature is depraved and spiritually dead; so that original sin may rightly be regarded as twofold, imputed sin and inherent hereditary sin.[28]

You may be tempted to think that this is all very academic, and amounts to no more than theological hair-splitting. In fact, it is a very serious theological matter for one simple reason: according to the New Testament, the basis of my condemnation as a sinner, and the basis of my justification in Christ are one and the same: union with my covenant representative. The parallel between Adam and Christ is foundational: 'as in Adam all die, so also in Christ shall all be made alive' (1 Cor. 15:22). Christ is described as the 'Second man' and the 'last Adam' (1 Cor. 15:45–49). It is as if only these two men ever existed, and our eternal destiny depends on our relationship to them. In the same manner in which we were lost—through the (immediate) imputation to us of Adam's sin and guilt—we are saved, through the (immediate) imputation of Christ's obedience and righteousness.

Ted Donnelly expresses it with beautiful simplicity when he says:

> We are saved in the same way as we were lost. Our redemption, though infinitely greater than our ruin, is in this respect parallel to it. In Adam we sinned. In Adam we fell. In Adam we were condemned. In Adam we died. And then in Christ we obeyed. In Christ we lived a perfect life. In Christ we paid for sin. In Christ we have been raised. In Christ we live forever.'[29]

The word 'impute' and related words appear in the Bible, and are the basis of our theology. But there are other words, like 'Trinity', 'incarnation' and 'supralapsarianism' which theologians will use which are not explicitly Scripture words. Theology is the science of expressing the thoughts and teachings of the Bible in the most precise and helpful form of words, even if these words themselves are not found in Scripture.

SIN'S EXPRESSION IN HUMAN EXPERIENCE

How does the disease of sin manifest itself? Clearly, if all we have said about the Bible is true, then sin's manifestations are multi-faceted. Sin is present any time God's law is broken, or any time it is disregarded, or any time the opposite of what God requires is perpetrated. If God says—as he does in the first commandment—that we are to have no gods other than He, then we sin both by our failure to acknowledge Him as God, and by our idolatry. That raises many issues, because we can so easily create gods for ourselves, and manufacture idols of pop, of sport, of recreation. We can idolise family life, or pregnancy, or gay marriage, or our car. Idols run away with our affections, and they fill our lives. At one level idols have no real existence, but at another level they exist powerfully in the lives of people.

The ten commandments are not merely a set of rules. They provide us with a summary of all the moral and ethical standards of the Bible, and they cover all of life. To that extent they are actually a worldview, which demonstrates that all our relationships, both with God and with people, are moral issues. The way we live shows how seriously we understand the nature of sin, and that in turn shows how seriously we take God.

In Jesus' teaching in the Sermon on the Mount, he reminded his hearers that a merely external obedience to the demands of the commandments was not what God required. For example, on murder, Jesus quotes the rabbis of his day who took the sixth commandment ('You shall not murder', Exodus 20:13; Deut. 5:17) and who taught that a murderer was liable to be put to death. But then he went on to say that the commandment goes further, and searches our attitudes to those who worship with us; we are sinning if we bring offerings to God while at the same time angry with our brother (Matt. 5:22–24). Similarly, the seventh commandment ('You shall not commit adultery', Exodus 20:14; Deut. 5:18) implies that we are sinning when lust rises up unchecked in our heart. Jesus is not redefining sin; he is reminding us that the implications of the law, and therefore the expressions of sin are much more extensive than we sometimes care to admit.

The Westminster Assembly of the seventeenth century considered it necessary to teach the meaning of the commandments to people, and so included in its Catechisms an extensive treatment of the law of God. The Westminster Larger Catechism devotes 56 out of its 196 questions and answers—over a quarter—to expounding the nature of sin in terms of what each commandment requires and what it forbids. Some might think that's excessive, until you study the Assembly's careful exegesis. Under the duties required in the third commandment ('You shall not take the name of the Lord Your God in vain, Exodus 20:7; Deuteronomy 5:11), the Assembly suggests that any way in which God reveals himself should be reverently used in our conversations (Questions 112); to do otherwise is a sin. That includes using religion 'for sinister ends' or backsliding (Q 113).

Similarly, the fifth commandment, about honouring our parents, includes more than our obedience to our biological father and mother—it has implications for all those who have positions of superiority 'whether in family, church or commonwealth' (Q124). The ninth commandment ('You shall not bear false witness', Exod. 20:16, Deut. 5:20), forbids anything that prejudices the truth, not least in courts of law; it forbids remaining silent when sins are being committed, and it forbids 'raising false rumours' (Q145).

The point is that the law is comprehensive in its scope. Sin finds expression in all our relationships in life. When our hearts and affections are not primarily set on God, when we worship God more to please ourselves than him, when we treat his name and word without reverence or respect, when we mismanage our time and use our days for our own ends, when we fail to honour and respect the different tiers of authority over us, when we do not hold life as sacred from conception to death, when we redefine marriage, when we take what is not ours, when we bend the truth to serve ourselves, when we desire something inordinately that belongs to someone else—in all of this sin finds expression.

It finds expression in our handling of relationships, in our handling of creation, in our mismanagement of time. It is expressed in thoughts, words and actions. No level of our lives is immune from the disease of sin. That is why

> When you think of the word 'sin', what do you think of? What is the popular notion of sin in our culture? There is always the danger that we confine the concept to actions and habits which spoil the environment, or threaten relationships, without probing into the reason for these actions. Sin is always more than sinful things.

we require to defer to God's definitions, not to decide ourselves what is right and what is wrong. Godless morality is a myth. Ironically it only leads to more rules, as a society without God tries to defend everyone's rights and ends up defending no-one's.

SIN'S EFFECTS IN HUMAN EXPERIENCE

If this is true, what, then, are the consequences of sin in our experience? What are the effects of the disease?

The most generic answer to that question is to say that sin results in death. The threat which God made to man's disobedience was the threat of death (Gen. 2:17). That threat was realised as soon as the covenant was broken, and Adam and Eve disobeyed God. The consequence of their disobedience, therefore, had a twofold effect, one on God and one on themselves.

As far as God was concerned, he responded to their sin with swift determination and faithfulness to the word he had previously spoken. Although his response to their sin was tempered with justice and grace, God did not deviate from what he had threatened. There is an element of punishment in God's response, because he cannot turn a blind eye to sin. Yet his relationship with the world, and with man and woman in it, is also modified. Death is the wages of sin (cf. Romans 6:23), but Adam is allowed to live physically, and to procreate. The seed of the woman will actually be the means of ultimate deliverance (Gen. 3:15). So Bavinck says:

> All the consequences and punishments that went into effect after the entry of sin, accordingly, from that moment display a double character. They are not merely the consequences and punishments appointed by God's justice but, from another perspective, also all without exception appointed means of grace, proofs of God's patience and compassion.[30]

God's patience modifies God's punishment, but it does not change it. In Genesis, the immediate effect of the fall is that man is driven out of the garden, and it is impossible that he should return to the paradise that he has lost. That effect continues to be experienced by us in original sin; we too are lost, and at the point of our origin we are outside God's Paradise. We are 'far off' from God (Eph. 2:13), and we continue to wander into the far country (Luke 15:13ff).

At this level, sin is its own punishment. Both guilt and corruption adhere to us as the threatened penalty of the covenant, and they inhere in us as constituent elements of our existence. More than that, it is possible for God to punish sin with more sin, such as when God punishes David's sin against Uriah and Bathsheba with the prospect of incestuous behaviour on the part of his children, or threatens our idolatry with a judgement of homosexual behaviour (Rom. 1:24–26). Francis Turretin discusses this theme of sin as its own punishment at great length, reminding us that sin is 'illegal in reference to the command of the law' yet 'legal in relation to the sanction of the law'... there is nothing to prevent God's avenging the injury done towards him by another injury, which he by a most wise and just judgement permits to be done to the injury of the creature.'[31]

But there are other effects of sin in our experience. Guilt, for example, is something we all feel when we sin. We know we have done wrong, and we instinctively sense that we are answerable and ought to be punished. It is both objective—in the sense that we are truly guilty whether we feel it or not—and subjective, for it registers itself in the depth of our being. We can quieten our conscience, and we can ignore it, but we cannot give it any peace until we know that God, in Christ, has forgiven our sin. As Herman Bavinck reminds us, 'guilt and the consciousness of guilt are not the same'[32], but the latter can often be a means towards dealing with the former.

Coupled with the awareness of guilt are the sense of shame and the sense of fear. Adam and Eve experienced these when the voice of God called to them out of the garden, and their instinct was to hide themselves from the presence of God. They were aware that they had sinned, and they neither wished their sin to be exposed, nor themselves to come as sinners into the hands of God. The same feelings of disquiet and of shame are effects of sin in our experience too.

A second effect of sin is bondage. Part of the worldview of the Bible is that a consequence of the Fall is that the world lies under the power of the evil one (1 John 5:19), who is called the prince of this world (John 12:31). Regeneration is described as a deliverance from the kingdom of darkness to the kingdom of the Son of God (Col. 1:13). When Jesus declared that his hearers were slaves to sin and Satan, they objected that they were the children of Abraham and not enslaved to any (John 8:33). Their very objection to Christ's teaching and their subsequent violence towards him (John 8:59) only demonstrated the truth of what he said. The work of God's grace is a work of emancipation, delivering us from the bondage of sin and Satan: 'Redemption in Christ is, in the first place, liberation from the devil' (Bavinck, vol 3, p. 187).

A third effect of sin is suffering. We are living in a world in which we experience pain, futility, uncertainty, bereavement and grief. It is a world that groans, waiting eagerly for its liberation (Rom. 8:20–23). Many of the Psalms of the Old Testament are psalms of lament and longing, and they register, to use the taxonomy of Walter Brueggemann, the Old Testament scholar, 'orientation, disorientation and reorientation.'[33] The doctrine of sin is an explanation for the disordering of things in our world, and for the sense of disorientation we feel when things go badly wrong.

That does not mean, of course, that every experience of suffering may be directly attributable to a particular sin. That is one of the great lessons of the Book of Job, in which a righteous man suffers, only to hear his friends argue that there must be some particular sin in his past which has occasioned such suffering. Their theodicy (their attempt to explain suffering) ultimately fails because they have failed to see the many purposes of God even in suffering. Yet there is no doubt that God has brought the 'evil' upon Job with an ultimate purpose of blessing

(Job 42:11–12). Job is caught up in the matrix of suffering that has entered the world on the back of sin.

John Murray uses the language of 'revolution' to describe this. Sin, he says, 'is a movement in the realm of spirit. But it drastically affects the physical and non-spiritual. Its relationships are cosmic.'[34] There is a 'cosmic revolution' expressed in the threat of God upon the ground, with the thorns and thistles it is to bear; but that is followed by a 'revolution in the human family,'[35] in which all of man's relationships are distorted and disorientated. We suffer in relationships as well as in earthquakes because of our sin. After the fall, humans remained human, animals remained animals, and the earth remained the earth. But 'nature gradually became degraded and adulterated.'[36] Sin created no new species, and was not some alien substance that entered into our experience, but it did open the door to a degeneration both of man's environment and of man's happiness. Sin is what makes us sad.

And, fourthly, sin is ultimately what kills us. Although the threat of death was not fully realised after the fall, man did experience a separation from God in the realm of the spirit, losing communion with God and the enjoyment of God's presence. It is one reason for the discontentment of a culture that has everything and nothing at the same time. Sin reverses God's order, breaks down God's distinctions, removes God's boundaries, and leaves man saying that 'all is vanity and a striving after wind' (Eccles. 2:17).

But that separation continues in two other modes: as a consequence of sin there is physical death and eternal death. Physical death is the dissolution of our nature, the separation of body and soul; eternal death is the eternal separation of man from God in a lost eternity, in which 'the restraints of the present fall away, and the corruption of sin has its perfect work.'[37] That is the most solemn, and most difficult to conceptualise, effect of sin in our experience.

In fact, it is so difficult that many have denied it altogether. The concept of an eternity of lostness and of separation from God in the torments of hell offends the sensibilities of fallen man, and even the sensibilities of theologians. 'I believe,' writes John Wenham, 'that endless torment is a hideous and unscriptural doctrine which has been a terrible burden on the mind of the church for many centuries and a terrible blot on her presentation of the gospel. I should indeed be happy if, before I die, I could help in sweeping it away.'[38] Wenham prefers to speak of 'conditional immortality', which assumes that death means annihilation and destruction, and endless life is the lot only of those who believe.

Yet this cannot do justice to the full weight of the biblical doctrine. Sin's repercussions and effects are eternal, for the offence of sin is against an eternal God. Annihilationism is not in any meaningful sense a more palatable doctrine than the traditional doctrine of conscious eternal punishment, for it cannot do justice to the biblical language. In Matthew 25:41, for example, 'the fire prepared for the devil and his angels' is eternal in consequence and duration.

There is no escaping the Bible's teaching that without faith in Jesus Christ, we are exposed to the full effects of sin in our experience—to guilt, bondage, suffering and to hell itself. Yet we do well to heed Wayne Grudem's point that 'if our hearts are never moved with deep sorrow when we contemplate this doctrine, then there is a serious deficiency in our spiritual and emotional sensibilities.'[39]

The doctrine of hell is one of the most unpalatable doctrines of our day. Liberalism has tried to extinguish the thought of it; modern preaching tends to downplay the seriousness of it. Jesus did not come to save us from hell, but to save us from sin. In doing so, he saves from all its consequences, including eternal destruction in hell.

How does the experience of Christ on the cross enable us to understand the experience of a lost eternity in hell?

Have we lost our sense of the urgent need of the gospel in the light of what is on the other side of death?

How should preachers communicate this doctrine?

THE SCOPE OF SIN IN HUMAN EXPERIENCE

How widespread is the disease? Is it something that just affects part of our being? Is it a matter of ethics and behaviour? Is the importance of the doctrine of sin that it affects the things we do and say?

Actually, the teaching of Scripture is much more radical than that. It is that sin *inheres* in us, that is, it is present in every aspect of our human make up and pyschology. This was a point that Augustine laboured in his treatment of original sin; 'infants,' he says, 'though incapable of sinning, are yet not born without the contagion of sin.'[40] The disease is present before its symptoms manifest themselves. As Thomas Boston says, dealing with the corruption of our nature and its manifestation in our children, 'It may soon be discerned what way the bias of the heart lies.'[41] Further, Augustine argues, it requires the grace of God in the new birth to remove the power that sin has from the point of our natural origin: 'in this condemned stock carnal generation holds every man; and from it nothing but spiritual regeneration liberates him.'[42]

This doctrine is referred to as the doctrine of 'total depravity', sometimes referred to as 'radical depravity'. It is concerned not so much with 'the extent of (man's) guilt before God, but the extent of his corruption in sin.'[43] Into what faculties of the soul has the pollution spread? The answer is—into all.

Perhaps we can approach this subject from another angle. Jesus summarises the requirement of the law of God in the following terms: 'You shall love the Lord your God with all your heart and with all your soul and with all your mind and with all your strength' (Mark 12:30, quoting Deuteronomy 6:4–5). The work of the Spirit of God in those who are born again is precisely this: to enable them to love God with their affections (heart), to love him spiritually (soul), to love him intellectually (mind) and to love him physically (strength). It would be difficult to find four more suitable words to express the totality of our human experience than these. Man is made to love, wired for spiritual things, able to reason and to cogitate, and endowed with physical strength. The claim of God's law is that in those areas and with these means we are to express our love for God.

Total depravity means that sin has infected and affected these root traits of our human nature. It has affected our hearts. We make the object of our affections and loves something other than God. God is love (1 John 4:8), and having been made in his image, we are capable of loving too. But instead of making God the supreme object of our affections, we set our heart on lesser things. We love the world, which is passing away, instead of God, whose will is the path to life (1 John 2:15–17). We turn love—which seeks the good of another—into lust—which seeks our own good. And sometimes God judges the sin of our hearts by leaving us to ourselves; the hardening of Pharaoh's heart is ascribed both to Pharaoh himself and to God, God judicially dealing with Pharaoh by leaving him to his own heart impulses (Exod. 8:15; 9:7, 12). In the same way, Paul tells us that God can give us up to our own lusts (Rom. 1:24).

We are told to guard our hearts, for the springs of life come from it (Proverbs 4:23). The words of God are to be in our heart (Deut. 6:6), and only those with a clean heart can come to God (Ps. 24:4). The covenant that God makes with us in these days is inscribed on our hearts (Jer. 31:33). The heart is the heart of the matter as far as the Bible is concerned; but tragically sin has infected our hearts. Ezekiel strikingly draws our attention to this when he says that we need our natural, stony heart to be removed, and we require a warm, fleshy heart to be given to us (Ezekiel 36:26). The disease of the heart is what will affect and infect the whole of our being and personality.

Coupled with this is the emphasis on the soul. That is the 'religious' element of our nature: our capacity for faith and worship. The root sinfulness of our heart will spill over into the arena of worship. Calvin captures this brilliantly when he says that the heart of man is 'a perpetual factory of idols'[44]; although we were made in the image of God, with a call to worship God alone, our hearts create new objects of worship. That is both a sin and the evidence of sin. It means that we all, whoever we are, are instinctively and intuitively religious; the problem is that we do not all, nor do we always, focus our soul's attention on the God who made us.

Third, total depravity means that sin affects our *minds*, our processes of reason and our logical thought. Professing ourselves to be wise, we become fools (Rom. 1:22), and God can give us over to the debasement of our minds (Rom. 1:28), so that we do the things we ought not to do. Paul delineates the distinction between regenerate and unregenerate man in terms of the mind: 'to set the mind on the flesh is death, but to set the mind on the Spirit is life and peace. For the mind that is set on the flesh is hostile to God, for it does not submit to God's law; indeed, it cannot' (Rom. 8:6–7). Later in the epistle to the Romans, he equates the renewing of the mind with nonconformity to the world (Rom. 12:2); similarly in Ephesians 2:3 he equates our exposure to the wrath of God with our 'carrying out the desires of the body and the mind'. Our mind is 'hostile' to God, and leaves us alienated and evil (Col. 1:21). It is this radical sin, which leaves our mind in darkness, that means that we require the washing of regeneration, which alone can give us a mind that will understand, and that will enable us to 'seek for God' (Rom. 3:11).

Finally, total depravity means that the scope of sin is such that it affects our strength. Actually, it means that we are spiritually unable to do certain things. John the Baptist said it with clarity: 'A person cannot receive even one thing unless it is given him from heaven' (John 3:27). Paul also says that it is only by God's working in us that we can work in a way to please him (Phil. 2:13). It was when we were *weak* and *without strength* that Christ died for us (Rom. 5:6).

Not only does sin weaken us in our ability to perform, or even to receive, spiritual things; it means that our strength is used for sinful ends. We do what is wrong, to ourselves, to others and to our environment. We pour our energies into the creation of what will elevate ourselves and give us glory. Like the tower-builders of Babel in Genesis 11, we are all out to conquer Heaven by creating paradise for ourselves through social means, all from the ground upwards.

That is what makes godless politics, art, environmentalism, music, film-making and education, ultimately empty and devoid of purpose. We labour for what does not satisfy (Isa. 55:2). We build weapons of war at the expense of the earth's resources, then cry that we need to take care of our environment. Like Solomon, we make great works, build houses, parks, gardens and pools; we spend energy on looking after flocks and entertaining ourselves to death, but without God it is all 'a striving after wind', with nothing to be gained under the sun (Eccles. 2:4–11).

The result of grace, however, is that we can, in fact, love God with all our strength. Our resources can be put to good use when we learn to pray 'Thy will be done' (Matt. 6:10). Only when our will is aligned with that of God, so that our heart, soul, mind and strength love him, will we be delivered from the bondage to sin that lies at the heart of our fallen human experience.

As theologians often remind us, 'total depravity' does not mean that we are as evil as we could be. The world would be uninhabitable were that the case. It is a way of expressing the fact that, at root, there is no aspect of our being which sin has not affected:

> having made due allowance for every single variation, for all the restraints of common grace, and for all the adornments of personality which we find in our human situation, it still remains that in every human being the totality of his humanness is affected by sin.[45]

GOD'S RESPONSE TO SIN IN HUMAN EXPERIENCE

We have already highlighted the way in which God responded to the Fall of Adam, with a word of judgement and curse. How could he not, when the terms on which he constituted man in relation to himself included the threat of death for covenant violation? God's judgements are in the earth still, so that he responds to sin in judgement, which means sometimes leaving us to our own sin, or exposing us to new sin as a judgement for old sin.

But the gracious aspect of God's self-revelation in Scripture is that there is mercy and forgiveness with God. If God should mark iniquity, who could stand? But with God there is forgiveness (Ps. 130:3–4). We can never presume on God's mercy; yet God's mercy is what is revealed to us. And, interestingly, we could never know of God's mercy apart from our sin. That does not justify sin; nor, indeed, does it justify mercy. But it does highlight the glory of God's grace, and the richness of God's mercy who, 'when we were dead in our trespasses, made us alive together with Christ' (Eph. 2:5). That mercy was revealed against the backdrop of our sin, and had to deal with our sin if we were to enjoy its benefits. For that to take place, God had to provide a remedy for our disease.

4

THE CROSS AND SIN

IS THERE A CURE?

The Puritan Richard Sibbes preached a sermon entitled 'Sin's antidote', which he based on the words of the institution of the sacrament of the Lord's Supper from Matthew 26:28, 'this is my blood of the covenant which is poured out for many for the forgiveness of sins.'[46] In it he makes the point that the first work of God's mercy is to forgive sins; everything is included in it. If our sins are forgiven, then all the blessings of God's grace are ours. The doctrine Sibbes draws from the text is that 'all the benefits that believers have by the new covenant, and so by the death of Christ, they are all of them given them in the remission (or forgiveness) of their sins.'[47] This, he adds, 'is the very key of the gospel'.

So the answer to our question is, 'Yes!' there is a cure for the disease of our sins, and it is inextricably bound up with the blood of Jesus which has been poured out for us on the cross. One of the earliest theological statements we have regarding the earthly ministry of Jesus is from John the Baptist, who pointed to Jesus and said 'Behold the Lamb of God, who takes away the sin of the world!' (John 1:29). John embodies the sweep of Old Testament prophecy at this point, and answers the question of Isaac as far back as Genesis 22:7, 'where is the lamb for the burnt offering?'. Abraham, his father, answers by saying that 'God will provide for himself the lamb for a burnt offering' (Gen. 22:8), a statement surely included in the claim of Jesus that Abraham saw the day of Christ (John 8:58).

Now the day of Christ has dawned, and the lamb has appeared 'to put away sin by the sacrifice of himself' (Heb. 9:26). It was specifically *for sin* that God sent his son into the world, in order to condemn sin (Rom. 8:3). The work of atonement was planned with sin in view; had there been no sin there would be no need for atonement. Jesus appeared 'in order to take away sins' (1 John 3:5), which is just another way of saying that those who are well have no need of a physician (Matt. 9:12); for why would he have to come as the remedy for our sickness if we were spiritually healthy?

But, as we have seen, we *are* in need of a physician. We are sick with sin; and it is precisely into this condition that the good news of salvation comes to us, saying to us that there is 'a balm in Gilead', and that there is a physician there (Jer. 8:22). There is a remedy for sin.

Regarding this remedy for our sins, we can say four things.

THE REMEDY IS DECLARED TO US IN THE GOSPEL

The gospel has no meaning apart from our condition as sinners and the effects of sin on us. If we are not sinners, we need no gospel. If there is no bad news about us, we don't need the good news of the gospel.

Yet there are many who preach the 'gospel' but who have little to say about sin. They are afraid that it is too negative to talk about sin; that it might even be rather offensive. Or they argue that the gospel presents a different kind of remedy—a remedy for physical sickness, or for material poverty. The message of the Bible can be twisted to address our apparent needs rather than our real need. We may feel that we need material prosperity and bodily health; and, if so, there are preachers who will tell vast audiences that God has promised these to his people. In fact he has not.

But what he *has* promised his people is a spiritual cure for spiritual problems, all of which are the result and the consequence of sin. This is the context into which we preach the gospel, and declare the good news. Of course, no amount of preaching can take the place of the work of the Holy Spirit, to whom it belongs to convict men and women of their sin and their need of righteousness (John 16:8–11). But neither can any amount of preaching the gospel have any lasting benefit unless we are convicted of our need, our sickness and our spiritual condition.

It was not, therefore, without reason that the Puritans laid special emphasis in their preaching on the law of God, as the means by which God brings home to sinners that they are, in fact, sinners. Joel Beeke summarises by saying that 'The Holy Spirit uses the law as a mirror to show us our impotence and our guilt, to shut us up to hope in mercy alone, and to induce repentance, creating and sustaining the sense of spiritual need out of which faith in Christ is born.'[48]

The Puritans did not teach that conviction is conversion. But they did teach that every one who is soundly converted to Christ has come to Him with a sufficient conviction of their need as sinners to 'flee for refuge to the hope set before us' (Heb. 6:18). That is the kind of evangelism we need: the evangelism that will show our need as sinners, and Christ's suitability as a Saviour.

'Puritans' is a name originally given as a nickname to the men and movements following the Reformation. Men like John Own, Thomas Goodwin, Richard Baxter and John Flavel were leading lights in the attempt to reform the church. They did not always share the same views on everything, but their theology and preaching was so Bible-focused and Christ-centred that they remain an important source for theology and preaching today.

THE REMEDY IS PROVIDED FOR US BY GRACE

There would be no gospel were it not for the grace of God. According to Paul, it is by grace that we are saved; and grace means that God's mercy toward us was rich, and his love toward us was great, precisely when we were dead in sins (Eph. 2:5).

Sometimes when tragedies occur we are prone to ask whether people deserved what happened to them. We have an instinctive idea that bad people deserve bad things, and good people deserve good things. But if God gave us what we deserved, we would be lost forever. 'Shall not the Judge of all the earth do what is just?' (Gen. 18:25). To ask the question is to answer it: God always does what is right. Yet he shows mercy, by not giving to us what we deserve; and he shows grace, by lavishing on us what we do not deserve. Because of his mercies, we are not consumed (Lam. 3:22, KJV). Because of his mercy, judgement is held back, and God is patient with us (2 Pet. 3:15). Because of God's mercy, even those who were the worst sinners can be saved; Paul's testimony was that 'though formerly I was a blasphemer, persecutor and insolent opponent…I received mercy because I had acted ignorantly in unbelief' (1 Tim. 1:13). Paul does not mean that his acting ignorantly in unbelief was the reason he received mercy; he means that, being at the very edge of God's patience, as his unbelief placed him, he nevertheless was within reach of the mercy of God.

So the gospel comes to us from the sovereign God who says that he will have mercy on whom he will have mercy (Rom. 9:15). He is not under any obligation to show mercy to any; but the gospel reveals him to be rich in mercy (Eph. 2:4; cf. Ps. 103:8, Ps. 145:8).

The other side of mercy is grace; not only does God not give us what we deserve, he gives us what we do not deserve. Grace can be seen only against the backdrop of sin; 'where sin increased, grace abounded all the more' (Rom. 5:20). Justification, the removal of the guilt and condemnation of our sin, is by God's grace (Rom. 3:24). Salvation from sin does not come about by our works, but only on the basis of God's grace (Rom. 11:6). The gospel is nothing other than the appearing of grace, bringing salvation for all people (Titus 2:11), and placing the remedy within their grasp.

The power of sin can only be broken by the power of grace. Often we confine our definition of grace to the favour which God shows us when we deserve something quite different. But grace is much more than a disposition of favour; it is the active work of God towards us, for us and in us, though we are spiritually dead. It is grace that raises the dead, moves the stubborn, seeks the lost and works the new birth. It is grace that makes the unwilling want to come to Jesus. It is grace that gives the unable the power to come to Jesus. It is grace that makes the self-centered focus on Jesus. The good news comes to lost, needy man as a gospel of grace.

THE REMEDY IS SECURED BY THE BLOOD OF JESUS CHRIST

Grace is free but not gratuitous. That is to say, it comes to us freely, offering us pardon, hope and new life in Jesus Christ. But these blessings were not secured without cost. That is the context in which Paul introduces the saving work of Jesus in Romans 8:3-4—it was on account of what the law could not do, because it was compromised by our sin and by our disobedience, that God, in grace, sent his Son to the world 'for sin'. If sin was to be dealt with, then atonement was necessary.

No book on the subject of sin can ignore what happened at Calvary. There, says Paul, God 'made him to be sin who knew no sin, so that in him we might become the righteousness of God' (2 Cor. 5:21). There are three great truths here.

First, there is the truth of *the sinlessness of Jesus*. Just as the passover lamb was to be 'without blemish, a male' (Exod. 12:5), so Jesus was to be without blemish and male. Actually, it was because Jesus was blameless and male that the lamb which typified him in the exodus drama had to carry these same qualities.

We have already noted that Jesus, as the embodiment of the law of God, was perfect and without sin. It was necessary that, as our sin-bearer, he should have no sins of his own for which atonement had to be made. The truth about Jesus is that he shed his blood 'like that of a lamb without blemish or spot' (1 Pet. 1:18). Even in the midst of the darkness of Calvary, Jesus was the light of the world, radiant in his holiness, unsullied and unstained by the sin and darkness all around him.

Second, there is the truth of *the imputation of our sins to Jesus*. Why, given that he had no sin, did Jesus have to shed his blood at all? What was it that made this necessary? And what made it possible?

What made it necessary was the very point Abraham pleaded before God in his intercession for Sodom: the

Judge of all the earth does what is right. Having opted to be merciful, God locked himself in to the provision of an atonement which would at once deal with man's need and not violate any of God's own attributes. He has purposed to show mercy to man, notwithstanding man's sin. But how can God do so without compromising his justice, or his own righteousness and integrity? It would be, by his own admission, as abominable to acquit the guilty as to condemn the innocent (Deut. 25:1). It is by the provision of a Saviour, in the person of his own Son, that the necessity of the atonement is realised, and God's integrity is maintained as his Son becomes his people's substitute.

But still the question remains: how is it possible that he is condemned to death? On a human level, the death of Jesus is itself a sin, a violation of every moral and ethical code of law. It was wrong. But on the level of God's mercy and grace, the death of Jesus is right: God deals with Jesus *for us*, as he carried our sins in his own body (1 Pet. 2:24), and was *made sin for us* (2 Cor. 5:21). Without that substitution, sin could never be dealt with. But through it, there is a balm provided for our guilt and our sin.

For that reason, John can argue our salvation not simply on the ground of God's grace and mercy, but on the grounds of God's *justice*; it is the blood of Jesus that cleanses us from sin, John says in 1 John 1:7; and if it is, then it is the justice of God that requires that God forgive the sins of those who confess them to him. God will condemn us if there is no substitute to take our place;

God will condemn the substitute if one is found. But God cannot, and therefore will not, condemn us having condemned the substitute. Sin is dealt with in the death of Christ once and for all.

THE COUNTER-IMPUTATION OF CHRIST'S RIGHTEOUSNESS TO US

This is how the death of Jesus, the last Adam, deals with the problem of our sin: by God, as a result of giving our sin to Christ to be condemned in his flesh, giving us his own righteousness, to allow us to stand before him in innocence and without blame. 'In him', in union with the Christ of the cross, we stand without condemnation. At Calvary, where our substitute stands, God sees us and condemns Him. Now, where we stand, God sees the righteousness of the substitute, and we are set free. None of the qualities of God are compromised; sin is dealt with fully and finally, and sinners are able to come finally before God. Sin once drove us out of Paradise;

As you reflect on the cross of Jesus, how do you answer these questions:
- **should Jesus have been crucified?**
- **was God present at the cross?**
- **why did Jesus not say 'My Father, why have you forsaken me?'**
- **did Jesus know who he was when he was shrouded in darkness?**
- **why was it a CROSS on which he died?**

now the Son has been driven out of Paradise precisely so that we may re-enter.

THE REMEDY IS RECEIVED BY FAITH

Just as surely as we are justified as a result of God's grace, and on the basis of Christ's blood, so we are justified by means of the faith that appropriates Christ's finished work to ourselves (Rom. 5:1). Faith leans on Christ and accepts the remedy of God's providing. It does not manufacture the remedy, or contribute to it in any way. It simply comes, knowing that Christ's blood is enough, and trusting that it is enough.

There is, therefore, in the Bible, always an antithesis between faith and sin. Paul states at the end of his discussion on not causing others to stumble that 'whatever does not proceed from faith is sin' (Rom. 14:23). Faith is always faith in the promise of God; sin is always a breach of the law of God. So what does not depend on the promise is a violation of the command. Similarly, Paul elsewhere argues that 'before faith came, we were held captive under the law ... the law was our guardian until Christ came, in order that we might be justified by faith' (Gal. 3:23–24). Whether Paul is to be interpreted as describing the history of redemption (the law of the Old Testament acting as guardian until Christ came in the fulness of time) or the application of redemption (the law dealing with us individually in conviction until faith in Christ justified us), the relative importance of faith and law in relation to each other is stressed. Where the law is broken, sin keeps us; only by faith can we be liberated from its curse, because faith rests on the word of covenant promise.

Of course, the opposite is also true. Where there is faith in the promise, there will be an antithesis against breaking the law. That is why Paul's argument in Romans moves swiftly from justification (how God deals with our sinful status) to sanctification (how God deals with our sinful condition). We do not continue in sin in order that grace might abound (Rom. 6:1–2). All that Jesus did for us was 'in order that the righteous requirement of the law might be fulfilled in us, who walk not according to the flesh but according to the Spirit' (Rom. 8:4). That antithesis is everywhere present: what is of faith is in opposition to what is of sin. All of which highlights the complexity of the man who is a Christian, who finds these contrary laws at work in his life (Rom. 7:19–20).

That complexity, however, belongs to the person who has found the answer to the question of sin, the solution to the problem, and the remedy for the disease: it is found in Jesus Christ, and in him alone. That is why the gospel is so precious in a world far away from God: there is a fountain, opened for sin and for uncleanness (Zech. 13:1), and it is at a place called Calvary, where Jesus died.

5

THE CHRISTIAN AND SIN

APPLYING THE REMEDY
WHILE LIVING WITH THE DISEASE

> O perfect redemption, the purchase of blood!
> To every believer the promise of God;
> the vilest offender who truly believes,
> that moment from Jesus a pardon receives.

So wrote Fanny Crosby (1820–1915) in one of the great evangelical hymns of the Christian tradition, entitled 'To God be the Glory'. The great truth of this second stanza is worthy of resounding praise and honour being given to God: when a sinner believes in Jesus, his or her sin is dealt with fully and finally. The antidote to sin has been applied, and the cure effects a change, a transformation in the diseased soul.

This application of redemption is all of grace, just as the need is all of sin. The disease is all ours; the remedy all God's. And just as surely as grace accomplished a perfect redemption in the atoning work of Jesus, so grace applies a perfect cure, and deals with the effects of sin in our experience.

That means that the cure must be at least equal to the disease, able to deal with its cause and with its effects. But more is necessary, because I want to make sure that this disease is prevented from doing any further damage. I don't want just to be brought back to the point from which Adam fell; I want to be placed where Adam would have been placed had he obeyed God and not fallen at all.

And that is what God does when he saves a sinner. The teaching of the New Testament is that the complexity of sin has been dealt with by a complex and multi-faceted salvation, all of which is given over to the believer in union with Jesus Christ. It is in him that we are complete (Col. 2:10, KJV), and it is in him that we have 'all things that pertain to life and godliness' (2 Pet. 1:3). All that sin took away, grace restores, and more besides. So when I believe in Jesus, there are at least ten things that occur.

First, *my bondage to sin is broken by the dominion of grace*. It is because of the dominion and domination of sin that we are by nature both unable and unwilling to come to Jesus. But freedom in Christ means, first, that our spiritual bondage is removed; God works in us, 'both to will and to work for his good pleasure' (Phil. 2:13). He makes his people willing to serve him, in a day of his own power (Ps. 110:3). Like Lazarus emerging from the grave, there must be a power at work in our lives greater than the power holding us in sin's bondage, chains and death. Indeed, the New Testament teaches us that the power by which we become Christians is nothing short of resurrection power; the same energy and potency by which Jesus was raised from the dead is the power that is at work in us (Eph. 1:19–20).

From this perspective, Paul can argue that our union with Christ is such that having died with him, we are also raised with him; and as death has no more 'dominion' over Christ once the resurrection takes place, so sin has no more dominion over us once we are made alive spiritually. This is not a matter of experience or feelings; it is a matter of fact, which we must believe in the light of God's word: 'you also must consider yourselves dead to sin and alive to God in Christ Jesus' (Rom. 6:11).

Second, *my guilt in sin is dealt with by my being justified*. It belongs to the complexity of our sin that it leaves us guilty, and open to condemnation. There cannot be law-breaking with impunity; where the law has been broken, sentence follows, and punishment is meted out. Otherwise the integrity of the law is in question. The God of the Bible 'is slow to anger and abounding in steadfast love, forgiving iniquity and transgression, but he will by no means clear the guilty....' (Num. 14:18). And there is the mystery of grace; in the application of redemption all these attributes are honoured: God does not clear our guilt, but imputes it to Christ; then, in steadfast love he forgives our sin and imputes Christ's righteousness to us.

Clothed in that alien righteousness, God upholds justice by pronouncing that in Christ Jesus there is no more condemnation (Rom. 8:1); we have been justified freely by his grace (Rom. 3:24). That is the aspect of redemption that deals with our native and inherent guilt: In Christ God justifies the ungodly who believe in Jesus, and shows the uprightness of his own nature by doing so.

Third, *my estrangement and lostness in sin are dealt with by my being adopted into God's family*. From the outset it was shown that sin leads to banishment. Adam and Eve were expelled from Paradise (Gen. 3:23), and ever since sin has left us estranged from God. The curse of the covenant is often expressed in terms of being 'cut off' from God, which is why circumcision in the Old Testament is such a powerful sign and symbol of the covenant. The 'cutting off' of the flesh corresponds to what sin does to us; but it also corresponds to what grace does to us, because it is by cutting off our sin that we are brought back into the bond of the covenant. That is why the grace of God is expressed in the arresting language of circumcision: 'the Lord your God will circumcise your heart and the heart of your offspring, so that you will love the Lord your God with all your heart and with all your soul, that you may live' (Deut. 30:6).

So when my sin cuts me off from the fellowship of God, with its potential to banish me from God's presence forever, grace brings me near (cf. Eph. 2:17–19). There is no more distancing. Christ was 'cut off' in our place and on our behalf, made a curse for us, in order to bring us to God. When this redemption is applied to us, we actually then have access into grace (Rom. 5:2).

Fourth, *my sinful nature is dealt with by the miracle of regeneration.* The miracle of grace is not simply that it means a legal change of status through adoption; it does what ordinary adoption cannot do: it actually gives me the nature of the family into which I am now brought. I remain the person I always was, but in Christ I am a new creation (2 Cor. 5:17), born again, that is, born from above (John 3:7). Peter draws this conclusion powerfully in his first epistle, where he says that God's people have been both redeemed objectively (1 Pet. 1:18) and then regenerated subjectively (1 Pet. 1:23), with the result that they have become spiritual people, nourished by spiritual milk (1 Pet. 2:2). All the teachings of the New Testament on what it means to become a Christian have their focus on the change that God works in human life.

Fifth, *my sinful and darkened mind is dealt with by the light of truth.* Sin casts a shadow into our powers of reasoning and logic; we were once 'alienated and hostile in mind' (Col. 1:21) as far as God was concerned. But now our minds have been set on spiritual things (Rom. 8:6), so that by the renewal of our minds our whole lives can be transformed (Rom. 12:2).

Sixth, *my stubborn, sinful, disobedient will is dealt with by God's effectual call.* There is an unwillingness and an inability to please God that is the hallmark of the unregenerate person; those who are in the flesh do not please God, nor can they, nor do they wish to do so (Rom. 8:8).

But God works in the lives of his people so that they actually want to please him; because they belong to God's flock they listen to him and follow him (John 10:27). God's calling of them lies at the heart of their salvation (Rom. 8:28, 30). Not to put too fine a point on it, the reason a sinner like me now calls on Jesus is because God first calls me (cf. 1 Cor. 1:2).

Seventh, *my sinful inclinations are dealt with through the giving of a new heart.* The older covenant spoke of this: God gives me a heart of flesh instead of the old heart of stone (Ezek. 36:26). Ezekiel's vision was not only of a restoration of God's people to Jerusalem out of captivity; he takes this as a metaphor for the spiritual emancipation from bondage that is at the very heart of our experience of grace. He will give a new Spirit to his people, so that they will obey him (Ezek. 36:27). Jeremiah's vision of the new covenant includes God writing of the law on the hearts of his people (Jer. 31:33, Heb. 10:16). Not only do they obey him now whereas they did not before; they want to do so. The new heart beats to the rhythms of grace in the gospel.

Eighth, *my sinful unbelief is dealt with through the giving of a new faith principle in my life.* Faith is the principle by which God's people live (Rom. 1:17, citing Hab. 2:4). It is not by faith they are saved, but by the grace which works through faith; the faith itself being a gift of grace (Eph. 2:8). This is not to detract in any way from the responsibility of men and women to respond freely to the offer of salvation in the gospel; quite the contrary. The God who makes salvation known in terms of a full and free gospel invitation is the God who is able to give the faith required to embrace Jesus. Men and women of faith do not become such because of the outworking of some undefined religious principle; they are made such by the inworking of the Spirit of God. Whereas sin kept our vision within the boundaries of what is 'seen and transient', faith enables us now to live by things that are unseen and eternal (2 Cor. 4:18).

Ninth, *my ongoing tendency to sin is dealt with by the work of sanctification.* God promises to make his people holy, and he asks his people to live holy lives. Christ died for our holiness (Eph. 5:26; Heb. 13:12) and prays for it (John 17:17). We will return to this in a moment, but the point to note is that sin does not disappear the moment we are born again; its dominion is broken and its penalty removed from us, but its presence and power still insinuate themselves and reveal themselves in our heart and life. The work of salvation is equal to this too. Grace does not deal simply with sins in the past, but sins in the present and in the future too. Christ is the antidote for all unrighteousness (1 John 1:9).

Tenth, *my security is guaranteed, so that no sin can separate me from the love of God in Christ.* The result of the original sin was to be disinherited from God. It belongs to the work of grace to restore what sin removed. But does my present sin and remaining corruption threaten the loss of the blessing and the life which are now mine in Christ? No, not at all; my inheritance is not only imperishable and undefiled, as Adam's was, but, unlike his, is also 'unfading' (1 Pet. 1:4). Sin caused my ruin, but will not be the cause of future ruin, for no-one can pluck me out of the Saviour's hand (John 10:28).

INDWELLING SIN

John 'Rabbi' Duncan used to talk about 'the chemistry of life that keeps us out of the range of the chemistry of death.'[49] That is what salvation is: it is the chemistry of life, and from it the chemist produces the antidote to all that is involved in the matrix of sin, condemnation and death. And, like every medicine, it begins its work immediately; but full health and recovery require a lifetime!

In other words, believing in Jesus means that I am perfectly saved, but does not mean that I am now perfect. As a Christian, I find myself dealing with sin and battling with it daily. In Martin Luther's words, I am '*simul iustus et peccator*': at the same time justified, yet a sinner. My identity in Christ is that I am righteous; as righteous, in fact, as I shall ever be! But my experience of Christ is that, clothed in his righteousness I still nevertheless find myself sinning. I want to be like Christ, but am often more like the world. I can backslide and wander far from God. I can become cold, and I can grieve the Holy Spirit.

The Heidelberg Catechism, Question 81, deals with the issue of who should come to the Lord's Supper and participate in it. The answer that is given is as follows:

> Those who are displeased with themselves because of their sins, but who nevertheless trust that their sins are pardoned and that their remaining weakness is covered by the suffering

and death of Christ, and who also desire more and more to strengthen their faith and to lead a better life. Hypocrites and those who are unrepentant, however, eat and drink judgment on themselves.

This summarises the spirituality that arose in the wake of the Reformation and continued into the Puritan era. It gives full place to the unity and sufficiency of the work of redemption for us and in us; but it also recognises that our experience of God's grace is such that we remain as displeased with ourselves as we are pleased with Christ, and we are aware of 'remaining corruptions' and weaknesses. Sin in the life of the Christian is an anomaly; after our union with Christ we live our lives accommodating a disease that is in the process of being eradicated—but which will not be fully removed until God takes us to glory. That means at least three things.

First, it means that day by day *we are aware of the presence of sin in our lives*. How can we not be? The great saints of the Bible acknowledge their sin before God— just look, for example, at the number of Psalms in which men of God acknowledge their folly: David in Psalm 51 and Asaph in Psalm 73, for example. Or read Romans 7, with Paul's great acknowledgement of two principles at work and at variance in his life, as he delights in God's law but is aware of another law working in his soul. Or the apostle John, who teaches us that no-one who is born of God makes a practice of sinning (1 John 3:9), yet who also says that if we have no sin we are deceiving ourselves (1 John 1:8).

But it is important to emphasise this because of the error of perfectionism which has appeared in the church from time to time, arguing that it is possible for us to reach a point in our Christian lives where we can live free from sin, either temporarily or permanently. Perfectionism is an error in the doctrine of sanctification; we know that God is making us holy, but is it possible for us to reach a point in our Christian lives where we sin no longer? Does the command to be perfect (Matt. 5:48) imply that we can, actually, be perfect in this life?

The concept of sinless perfection in this life appears occasionally in the church fathers (for example, Polycarp's letter to the Philippians contains the line that 'if anyone be inwardly possessed of these graces, he hath fulfilled the command of righteousness, since he that hath love is far from all sin.'[50] The Wesleyan tradition popularised this view in the eighteenth century.[51] Theologian Millard Erickson makes the general comment that 'Calvinists are usually nonperfectionistic' in their theology, while perfectionist theologies, such as are found in some Pentecostal groups, tend to be Arminian.[52]

The reality is, however, that while we do not live in sin (as the dominant force in our lives), sin does live in us. We recognise both the fact that sin no longer reigns, but that sin does still survive. And as Philip Ryken helpfully points out, 'It is just because we are free from sin that we must fight so fiercely against it.'[53] To claim perfection for ourselves while we are still in this world is probably itself a sin! 'It is the excellence of a holy man,' writes

Bishop Ryle, 'that he is not at peace with indwelling sin, as others are.'[54]

Second, it means that *we are set on putting sin to death*, on 'mortifying' the deeds of the body (Rom. 8:13; cf. Col. 3:5). This is a favourite theme in Puritan literature, where the battle against sin is seen as the key of the Christian life. In his extensive exposition of the meaning and practical application of Romans 8:13, the Puritan John Owen begins with his thesis that 'the choicest believers, who are assuredly freed from the *condemning* power of sin, ought yet to make it their business all their days to mortify the *indwelling* power of sin.'[55] This, he argues, belongs to the gift of Christ by his Spirit in the life of the child of God.

Such a warfare against ourselves requires knowing God, knowing ourselves, and knowing the nature of sin. It is at the cross we see what sin is, and what sin does. And it is the sin that effected the cross that lives in us still, with its will and power and tendency to crucify Jesus all over again in our own hearts. The only answer to that is that sin itself be crucified, which is the language Paul uses in Galatians 5:24—'those who belong to Christ Jesus have crucified the flesh with its passions and desires'. To continue with the analogy of this book, this is not 'self-medication' against sin; this is the very heart of the Christian life, in which sin's cure is entirely from Christ, and entirely engages the Christian who wants to become like Jesus.

The reality, of course, is that often Christians can lose these battles, even if they know that in Christ they have won the war. Christians can develop habits of behaviour that can turn into addictions and lead into temptation and sin. We all know of Christians who, even in their mature Christian experience, became addicted to alcohol, or to unhelpful online activities. We believe that those who are born of God do not keep on sinning (1 John 3:6). We wish we could be like Joseph in every situation of temptation and flee the scene saying 'How can I do this great wickedness and sin against God?' (Gen. 39:9). Often, however, we give in, and, like Peter denying Jesus, we do the very thing we insisted we would never do.

When we do find ourselves despairing of our apparent inability to win the battle with sin, we need to seek help from God, from Christian friends, and even from secular agencies who can help people who have developed unhealthy patterns of living. The one thing we must not do is ignore the very means and channels which God himself has provided for our growth in grace: keep praying, keep listening to the preaching of the Word, keep reading the Bible. These are the means which will enable us, whatever our personal failings, to keep our eyes on Jesus, our only hope.

Third, it means a continual repenting of the presence and activity of sin. None of what I have been saying is meant to be a counsel of despair; we battle against sin very imperfectly, and at times hardly at all. But the habit of repentance is a good one; indeed, it is the only avenue open to us day by day as we grow in awareness of our many imperfections. We live by faith in the Son of God who loved us and gave himself for us (Galatians 2:20), and accompanying our trust in him is our confession and our continual repentance. Which of us cannot resonate with the following prayer:

> There is no pardon but through thy Son's death,
>   no cleansing but in his precious blood,
>   no atonement but his to expiate evil.
> Show me the shame, the agony, the bruises of incarnate God,
>   that I may read boundless guilt in the boundless price;
>   may I discern the deadly viper in its real malignity,
>   tear it with holy indignation from my breast,
>   resolutely turn from its every snare,
>   refuse to hold polluting dalliance with it.
> Blessed Lord Jesus, at thy cross
>   may I be taught the awful miseries from which I am saved,
>   ponder what the word 'lost' implies,
>   see the fires of eternal destruction;
> Then may I cling more closely to thy broken self,
>   adhere to thee with firmer faith,
>   be devoted to thee with total being,
>   detest sin as strongly as thy love to me is strong,
>   and may holiness be the atmosphere in which I live.[56]

PERFECTION TO COME

This is not, however, the end: Christians do believe in perfection, just not yet! One day we shall be like Jesus, and see him as he is (1 John 3:2). The gospel hope is that all sin will be eradicated in a world in which perfection and righteousness alone will dwell (2 Pet. 3:13). There, 'no inhabitant will say "I am sick"; the people who dwell there will be forgiven their iniquity' (Isa. 33:24). In his work on Original Sin, Augustine reminds us that the children of those whose sins have been forgiven are themselves still guilty of sin, and adds that such will be the case 'until every defect which ends in sin by the consent of the human will is consumed and done away in the last regeneration.'[57] That is the hope by which we are saved: that all will issue at last in glorification, and 'the creation itself will be set free from its bondage to decay and obtain the freedom of the glory of the children of God' (Rom. 8:21). That, at last, and that alone, will be the restoration of Paradise. And sin will be gone forever.

6

EPILOGUE: WHAT'S THE USE OF SIN?

The doctrine of sin is a dark doctrine. It takes us to the very core of our being, and to our radical departure from God. It speaks in negative terms. Its tones are shadowy, its notes deep. It is not a user-friendly doctrine.

Indeed, for these reasons and more, some might say that it is a most unhelpful doctrine. Should we not major on the love of Jesus, the grace of God, the power of the Holy Spirit? Is all this talk about sin not just taking us back to Victorian moralism, to a legalistic, judgemental religion that is happy to point out how bad everything is and where everything is going wrong?

Is there any use in sin today? By which I don't mean whether there is any advantage to us sinning! There is not. By asking the question I am asking what are the practical reasons why a robust biblical doctrine of sin is necessary?

First, a doctrine of sin does justice to the Bible's revelation of God. There is a *theological* need to articulate the meaning of sin. Understanding sin helps us to see the glory of God, and in particular, the glory of God's grace and mercy towards us. Sin speaks about ourselves, but it throws into clear relief and focus all that God purposed to become for us in Jesus Christ. It is the dark background against which the glorious light of gospel truth shines and is seen in its incomparable beauty.

Second, a doctrine of sin helps us to explain what has gone wrong with the world. There is an *apologetic* value to it. It reminds us that this world ought to have been, and could have been, much better than it is. A doctrine of sin highlights that we are the problem, not anything outside of us.

And third, a doctrine of sin is necessary if we are to preach the gospel. There is an *evangelistic* value to it. The cross, Jesus, grace, God's love and mercy—none of these have any meaning apart from the fact of our spiritual need and enslavement to sin. We are called to witness to a remedy: Jesus loved us and gave himself for us. But the remedy is of no help unless we know the disease. In all our preaching and evangelism we are to show people what they are, but not so as to leave them self-focussed. Like the woman with whom Jesus engaged at the well in Samaria, we want people to say, 'Come see a man who tole me all that I ever did. Can this be the Christ?' (John 4:29). Then we want them to know all that the

Christ ever did, and continues to do, so that sinners like us can be saved.

Our need is great; that is what the doctrine of sin is saying. But there is an answer, and it is in Jesus Christ. That is what the gospel is saying.

ENDNOTES

1 John C. Lennox, *Gunning for God: Why the New Atheists are Missing the Target*, Lion Publishing, 2011, p. 113

2 See William VanDoodewaard, *The Quest for the Historical Adam*, Reformation Heritage Books, 2015

3 O. Palmer Robertson, *The Christ of the Prophets*, P&R Publishing, 2008, p. 93

4 B.B. Warfield, 'Jesus the Measure of Men' in *Selected Shorter Writings*, Vol 2, P&R Publishing, 2005, p. 687

5 'Tertullian Against Marcion', Book 2.6, in *Ante-Nicene Fathers*, Vol 3, p. 302

6 Ibid. 2.7, p. 303

7 Ibid. 2.9, p. 304

8 A.E. McGrath, *Christian Theology: An Introduction*, Blackwell, 2011, p. 223. See the discussion on pp. 223–7

9 John Calvin, Commentary on Genesis 45 in *Commentaries of John Calvin* vol 1, Baker, 2009, p. 377

10 Ibid., p. 378

11 G. Vos, *Reformed Dogmatics*, Vol 1, Hexham Press, 2015, p266

12 Herman Bavinck, *Reformed Dogmatics, Vol 3*, Baker Academic, 2006, p66

13 Ibid., p. 65

14 C. Van Dixhoorn, *Confessing the Faith*, Banner of Truth, 2014, p. 45

15 R.C. Sproul, *Truths we Confess*, Vol 1, P&R, 2006, p. 107

16 R.L. Dabney, *Systematic Theology*, Banner of Truth, 1985, p. 288

17 Douglas Moo, 'Sin in Paul', *Fallen: A Theology of Sin*, C.W. Morgan and R.A. Peterson (eds), Crossway, 2013, Kindle edition, loc 2351, accessed 5 May 2015

18 Jonathan Edwards, 'The Great Doctrine of Original Sin Defended', *The Works of Jonathan Edwards*, edited by E. Hickman, n.d. Vol 1, p. 192

19 W.G.T. Shedd, 'The Sinfulness of Original Sin' in *Sermons to the Natural Man*, Banner of Truth, 1977, p. 273

20 B.B. Warfield, 'Repentance and Original Sin' in *Selected Shorter Writings*, Vol 1, edited by J.E. Meeter, P&R Publishing, 2005, p. 279

21 W. Grudem, *Systematic Theology*, IVP, 2004, p. 1244

22 *The Works of Benjamin B. Warfield*, Vol 9: Studies in Theology, Baker Book House, 2000, p. 302

23 Bavinck, *Dogmatics*, Vol 3, p. 101

24 W.G.T. Shedd, *Dogmatic Theology*, Vol 2, Edinburgh, 1889, p. 185

25 Ibid., p. 188

26 Charles Hodge, *Systematic Theology*, Vol 2, London, 1888, p. 192

27 Ibid., Vol 2, p. 193

28 Canon XI, Formula Consensus Helvetica (1675), in *Reformed Confessions of the 16th and 17th Centuries in English Translation:* Vol 4, 1600–1693, J.T. Dennison jr (ed), Reformation Heritage Books, 2014, p. 523.

29 E. Donnelly, *Life in Christ*, Bryntirion Press, 2007, p. 19

30 Bavinck, *Reformed Dogmatics*, Vol 3, p. 160

31 F. Turretin, *Institutes of Elenctic Theology*, Vol 1, P&R Publishing, p. 656. The topic is discussed as topic 9, question 15, pp. 653–8

32 Bavinck, *Reformed Dogmatics*, Vol 3, p. 173

33 See for example, the introduction to W. Brueggemann, *The Message of the Psalms: A Theological Commentary*, Fortress Press, 1985

34 J. Murray, 'The Fall of Man' in *Collected Writings of John Murray*, Vol 2: Systematic Theology, Banner of Truth, 2009, p. 72

35 Id.

36 Bavinck, *Reformed Dogmatics*, Vol 3, p. 181

ENDNOTES | 101

37 Louis Berkhof, *Systematic Theology,* Banner of Truth, 2005, p. 261

38 J. Wenham, *Facing Hell: The Story of a Nobody,* Paternoster Press, 1998, p. 256

39 W. Grudem, *Biblical Doctrine: Essential teachings of the Christian Faith*, IVP, 1999, p. 461–2

40 Augustine 'On Original Sin', in Anti-Pelagian Writings, *Nicene and Post-Nicene Fathers*, Vol 5, T&T Clark, 1997, p. 252

41 T. Boston, *Human Nature in its Fourfold State*, Banner of Truth edition, p. 68

42 Augustine, id.

43 R. Phillips, *What's so Great about the Doctrines of Grace?*, Reformation Trust, 2008, p. 20

44 John Calvin, *Institutes of the Christian Religion,* 1.11.8)

45 D. Macleod, *A Faith to Live By*, Christian Focus Publications, 1998, p. 83

46 *Works of Richard Sibbes*, Vol 7, Banner of Truth, 2001, p. p261–79

47 Sibbes, 'Sin's Antidote', p. 268

48 J.W. Beeke, *Puritan Reformed Spirituality*, Evangelical Press, 2006, p. 103

49 John Duncan, *Colloquia Peripatetica,* Edinburgh, 1871, p. 47

50 *Ante-Nicene Fathers*, Vol 1, pp33–34

51 See Iain H. Murray's discussion of 'Christian Perfection' in Chapter 10 of his book *Wesley and Men who Followed*, Banner of Truth, 2003

52 M. Erickson, *Christian Theology*, Baker Academic, 1998, p. 984

53 P. Ryken, *The Message of Salvation*, IVP, 2001, p. 248

54 J.C. Ryle, *Holiness*, 1956, p. 38

55 J. Owen, 'Of the Mortification of Sin in Believers' in *Works of John Owen*, Volume 6, Banner of Truth, 2004, p. 7

56 *The Valley of Vision*, (A. Bennett ed), Banner of Truth, 2009, p. 183

57 Augustine, *Original Sin*, Vol 5, p. 253

FURTHER READING

J.R Beeke and M Jones (eds), *A Puritan Theology: Doctrine for Life*, Reformation Heritage Books, 2012, Chapter 13

Henri Blocher, *Original Sin: Illuminating the Riddle*, Paternoster, 1997

Iain D Campbell, *The Doctrine of Sin*, Mentor, 2009

Wayne Grudem, *Bible Doctrine: Essential Teachings of the Christian Faith*, IVP, 1999, Chapter 13

Donald Macleod, *A Faith to Live By*, Mentor, 2015, Chapter 8

C.W. Morgan and R.A. Peterson Fallen: *A Theology of Sin*, Crossway, 2013

John Owen, 'The Mortification of Sin in Believers', *Works of John Owen*, Vol 6, Banner of Truth, 2004 (for a modern edition of this work, see Kelly M Kapic and Justin Taylor (eds), *Overcoming Sin and Temptation*, Crossway, 2015).

Robert L Reymond, *A New Systematic Theology of the Christian Faith*, Thomas Nelson, 1998, Chapter 12

David L. Smith, *With Wilful Intent: A Theology of Sin*, Wipf and Stock, 2003

R.C. Sproul, *What can I do with my guilt?* (Crucial Questions Series), 2011

———, *Truths we Confess: A Layman's Guide to the Conferssion of Faith*, Vol 1, P&R Publishing, Chapter 6

Chad Van Dixhoorn, *Confessing the Faith: A Reader's Guide to the Westminster Confession of Faith*, Banner of Truth, 2014, Chapter 6

Other books in the Series:

A Christian's Pocket Guide to Jesus Christ
An Introduction to Christology
MARK JONES
ISBN 978-1-84550-951-4

A Christian's Pocket Guide to Baptism
The Water that Divides
ROBERT LETHAM
ISBN 978-1-84550-968-2

A Christian's Pocket Guide to Being Made Right With God
Understanding Justification
GUY WATERS
ISBN 978-1-78191-109-9

A Christian's Pocket Guide to Growing in Holiness
Understanding Sanctification
J. V. FESKO
ISBN 978-1-84550-810-4

A Christian's Pocket Guide to Loving the Old Testament
One Book, One God, One Story
ALEC MOTYER
ISBN 978-1-78191-580-6

A Christian's Pocket Guide to the Papacy
Its origin and role in the 21st century
LEONARDO DE CHIRICO
ISBN 978-1-78191-299-7

A Christian's Pocket Guide to Suffering
How God Shapes Us through Pain and Tragedy
BRIAN COSBY
ISBN 978-1-78191-646-9

Christian Focus Publications

Our mission statement –

STAYING FAITHFUL

In dependence upon God we seek to impact the world through literature faithful to His infallible Word, the Bible. Our aim is to ensure that the Lord Jesus Christ is presented as the only hope to obtain forgiveness of sin, live a useful life and look forward to heaven with Him.

Our books are published in four imprints:

CHRISTIAN FOCUS

Popular works including biographies, commentaries, basic doctrine and Christian living.

CHRISTIAN HERITAGE

Books representing some of the best material from the rich heritage of the church.

MENTOR

Books written at a level suitable for Bible College and seminary students, pastors, and other serious readers. The imprint includes commentaries, doctrinal studies, examination of current issues and church history.

CF4•K

Children's books for quality Bible teaching and for all age groups: Sunday school curriculum, puzzle and activity books; personal and family devotional titles, biographies and inspirational stories – Because you are never too young to know Jesus!

Christian Focus Publications Ltd,
Geanies House, Fearn, Ross-shire,
IV20 1TW, Scotland, United Kingdom.
www.christianfocus.com